EAST AFRICA IN THE FIFTIES

East Africa in the Fifties

A View of Late Imperial Life

S.J. Colman

Radcliffe Press
London • New York

Published in 1998 by
The Radcliffe Press
Victoria House
Bloomsbury Square
London
WC1B 4DZ

In the United States of America
and Canada, distributed by
St Martin's Press
175 Fifth Avenue
New York
NY 10010

A full CIP record of this book is available from
the British Library and the US Library of Congress

ISBN 1 86064 235 7

Typeset and designed by Dexter Haven, London
Printed in Great Britain by WBC Ltd, Bridgend, Mid Glamorgan

Contents

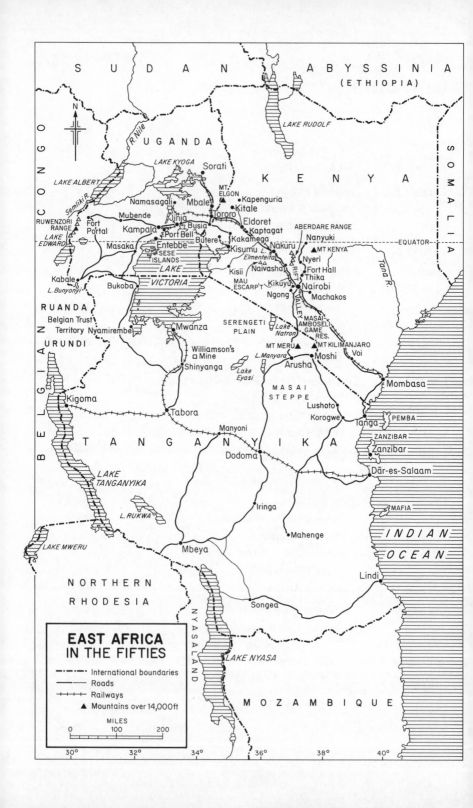

EAST AFRICA
IN THE FIFTIES

—·—·— International boundaries
————— Roads
+++++ Railways
▲ Mountains over 14,000ft

MILES
0   100   200

Preface

My wife and I decided in our twenties that for us the best form of travel was neither wild exploration nor tourism but to work somewhere away from home as privileged outsiders, to stay long enough to take a place with the people we lived among. I have set out here to recall our first such period of adventure by bringing to life the many aspects of what it was like for a young English family to live for six years in the East Africa of the fifties: that is, at almost the end of Empire there. So this is a travel book of sorts, about an epoch that, because long past but still close enough to be invisible, seems fictional to most readers today. Yet you might have come out to stay with us. You would have met all sorts of people of various races and tribes, heard the issues of that place and day discussed, sat out for tea in our shady, frangipani-scented garden, dipped into the gossip, gone on safari with us, wished you could stay longer. To adapt some words of Somerset Maugham's, by reading here in this hard world of today you too may come to look back upon the trivial with tender sympathy and even wring a delicate pathos from futility.

The late Margery Perham urged us to write such a book as this: otherwise, she feared, all our experience would be lost as colonial times slipped away into the past. Now that I have responded I have had to use the language and assume again the attitudes of 40 years ago. So to stumble into the dark backward is unavoidably risky if one's aim is to be truthful. I have done my best, at least, to leave the result uncensored by more recent general sensibilities or by the extent to which my own opinions have changed, as they have, in some ways fundamentally.

In those years there lived in British East Africa (the Uganda protectorate, Kenya colony and protectorate, the Tanganyika trust territory, and Zanzibar) 18 million Africans, in 64 main tribes. In general they survived precariously, their environment largely harsh. Far less numerous there than further south, in the Rhodesias or South Africa, other races amounted to 230,000 from India and Pakistan (rather less than half of them born in East Africa) and only some 45,000 from Europe. Taken together, the four distinct territories made up roughly the size of Europe west of the Oder.

Our friend Bernard de Bunsen, who appears here in several places, died in 1990. In the seventies he urged me to publish a full account of certain differences, in which we had together been deeply involved, that had arisen in the fifties between Makerere University College and the East African governments. For various reasons I had to disappoint him: now even the references in Chapters 8 and 10 are, sadly, too late for him.

Some of the people mentioned here were later given a new status and sometimes a new name in honours lists. To avoid confusion I have relegated all titles to the Index and left names as they were in East Africa. Similarly I have retained the names by which countries and places were known in the fifties.

My thanks go out to my old Makerere friends, colleagues and students. An unforeseen pleasure in writing this book has been to discover in my memory a throng of fascinating people, fresh-faced, lively with the beauty of youth (some, perhaps, a little more so than they could have been in fact), not ghostly but quick and present, ready to stand and talk out there on Makerere Hill in the brief, golden, equatorial evening. As my wife and I join in their conversation, this shining group in my mind contains impartially those still living and others now dead. That, come to think of it, is in harmony with the common pagan African belief that the departed attain whatever afterlife is theirs in survivors' memory of them, in particular of their names.

I offer loving thanks to our son Charles and daughter Julia, who were there too, for their prompting and suggestions. My main debt is to my oldest friend, my wife, for her sustained encouragement and invaluable memory in what has become a joint effort. We were there together and are together still to record it.

Chapter 1   The Arrival Not the Journey Matters

To have left England and be flying out to East Africa in March 1953 seemed a strange, possibly dubious, thing to be doing after such brief preparation. At Chipping Norton, admittedly, the wind had been in the habit of blowing cold across the valley from Stow-on-the-Wold's rooftops, visible up on the opposite crest, and straight through every firmly-closed door or window in our seventeenth-century farmhouse. In contrast, a glance at the *Encyclopedia Britannica*'s account of southern Uganda's climate had suggested an upland, equatorial paradise, warm the year round but not sweltering, with rainfall regulated into specific seasons and even then confined to only half of any day. Fertile soil, friendly people, an old hand had assured us, an excellent place for young children. For adults too? Such advantages, his manner had implied, exemplified the many virtues of a benevolently-governed British protectorate: "Happy Uganda", as the saying went. The very names, Kenya and Uganda (but not Zanzibar or Tanganyika, formerly German East Africa) had revived memories of Sunday school, of collections in support of the missions in those unimaginably distant, red places on the map. This was pocket money, we thought, for those other children, Africans, whose impenetrable photographs illustrated stories, meaningless to us, in the thin printed pamphlets we were given to take home.

Even so, there were other fragments, more disturbing, to fill those protracted pauses for doubt on the long flight. It was indisputably the case that Makerere College, the new University College of East Africa, had urgently requested our presence in Kampala. The Colonial Office in London had had excellent intentions when in 1950 it had transformed Makerere from a teacher training college into a university college affiliated with the University of London. We sympathised with such a chance of higher education for qualified students, almost entirely Africans, from all over East Africa. Recently, however, these newly privileged students had gone on strike, the sort of event that is apt to disturb authority whether benevolent or repressive. In some way (but how?) we were to improve conditions at Makerere. But what were they really like? Were we going so that the stability of paradise could be regained? After all, Winston Churchill, speaking in Uganda, had said, "I am amazed at the spectacle before me. Uganda, it seems, is like an island of light amid a sea of darkness."

Of course, that had been back in 1907, and even then there had already been others who had acknowledged the ruthlessly bloodthirsty despotisms of Uganda's recent pagan past. Now, in the fifties, just before we left, a friend had thoughtfully urged me to buy a pistol: "A Luger would be best, and always fire through the bedclothes, saves time, life or death."

He had had in mind the riots in Uganda in 1945 and 1949, and that in 1952 the first Mau-Mau murders of whites in Kenya had shocked even pro-African opinion. The Governor and Commander-in-Chief of that colony had put on his plumed hat to declare the State of Emergency, whereupon eleven Europeans had been killed out on their farms a couple of days later. A general call-up of white men had affected all from ages eighteen to forty. Another solicitous friend had enquired anxiously about our inoculations, warned against the slightest toleration of mosquitoes, and recommended a daily siesta, "But always put a towel over your middle: you'll be lying in the buff, you see, too hot for a sheet in the daytime." The penalty for forgetting his injunction was diarrhea.

Then there was the distressing fact that a member of the Makerere faculty, who had kindly met us for lunch in London during his leave and suggested we read Mannoni on the psychology of colonisation, a few days later had committed suicide. Even paradise must have its complications.

In any case, there we were up in the hands of the British Overseas Airways Corporation and about to find some answers to our questions.

Well, not soon. We had just left Cairo where our infant son, Charles, had at last fallen asleep. A thousand miles ahead of us lay another refuelling stop, at Khartoum. There we would drink a sticky liquid of repulsive sweetness and feel a punch of heat as the enormous ball of fire burst upon another day. Entebbe, the seat of Uganda's colonial government, would then lie well over a further 1,000 miles to the south. Plenty of time to reflect fruitlessly on all that might await us. But why bother? When I had responded to an advertisement in *The Times* for the vacant post of warden of Northcote Hall, Makerere's large new students' residence for men, I had had no clear idea of what I should be doing were I appointed. Nor had Frank Jessup, Secretary to Oxford University's Delegacy for Extra-Mural Studies (I was one of its tutors, as was my wife before our son's birth). In seeking his advice I had been staying within a familiar general context: for some time the Delegacy had been sending its staff out to Africa, although hitherto exclusively to the West Coast. Frank had said that if I insisted on leaving for Makerere he would support me strongly, but they would be lucky to get me. Had he known something about Makerere that we did not?

The ensuing interview at the Inter-University Council for Higher Education in the Colonies had been mystifyingly desultory, in fact seemed hardly to have happened. No mention of the students' strike, of which we were to learn later. While I had been left to believe that Carr-Saunders, chairman of the Inter-University Council, had pronounced us the right stuff for this nebulous job – he should know? – a stronger impression had been that all would be decided by whatever the Principal of Makerere, Bernard de Bunsen, might think of me, and he had been expected in London shortly. When everything had seemed to fall quiet Bernard himself had telephoned: he would like to call on us at Chipping Norton (no doubt on the excellent principle of interviewing the family as well as the candidate). I had promptly invited him to lunch.

On the day he had arrived punctually, had been typically (as we were to learn) both genial and watchfully reserved, authoritative yet diffident, had spoken vaguely but encouragingly of difficulties at Makerere, and by the time he left had made it clear that he had given me the job, one which remained enticingly undefined. Evidently we had got on, but which of our supposed merits had persuaded him? Had it been our modest staff of nursemaid, gardener, and the daily help? Such matters, we gathered from him, could be of great import, for some British families in East Africa found themselves for the first time in their lives with servants. Some such, his suggestion was tentative but unmistakable, had an unfortunate tendency to conduct themselves in a manner that he considered not exactly conducive to good relations with Africans. That was a point that led us to speculate at length, later, on what sort of goings on these could be. But then, perhaps Bernard's mind had been made up by his long trek before lunch to our lavatory, up the back staircase past chilly, north-facing Edwardian bedrooms of spartan good character, with their sober walnut furniture.

Who can tell what circumstances, trivial to some but illumination to the wise, make up minds to entrust this person, not that, with an appointment? He had certainly beamed as he came down. Could it be that methods of divination available only to initiates had been secretly invoked? The trouble with inspecting entrails or other arcane procedures was that history seemed to be littered with their failures: fleets lying lost on the crawling bottom of the Mediterranean, along the Rhine the bones of slaughtered legions. (When in 1956 I was appointed Director of Extra-Mural Studies at Makerere, the selection procedure was even more informal. One morning, before 7.30, Bernard simply walked down without warning to my office in Northcote Hall. Both freshly shaved, fed and rested, we looked at each other enquiringly. Then after a few preliminaries he asked me to take the job.)

With fatigue feeding fantasy we droned on towards Entebbe. There at last, as we came in, was the huge horizon of Africa's largest lake, Victoria, about the size of Scotland, we had read, but not the shape, and at 3,717 feet above sea level. Suddenly hope revived. We became positively Stanleyish, or as though abruptly converted to a reverse Taoism: the arrival not the journey matters. Where all had been reasonable doubt, now everything seemed unreasonably possible, no matter how unknown: away with caution, we were only thirty-one. Deaf from the flight, we stood almost at the equator on this best of sunlit afternoons, with the clocks at GMT plus three hours. Since Uganda was a British protectorate, we needed no passports to enter it. As we came out of the airport we stopped to observe our new life's first detail, iridescent humming birds hovering to feed from hibiscus flowers in the thin strip of dusty garden.

Soon we were leaving lakeside Entebbe: our first close encounter with the rest of paradise was disconcerting. Nobody had told us that its soil was red; or that it had the hot and humid smell of rotting

4

vegetation. We were inappropriately dressed, admittedly, in our English clothes (could this other odd smell arise from a suit already mildewed?) but along the 20 or so miles to Kampala the Africans by the roadside looked as steamed and dispirited as we were beginning to feel. Set back a few steps on their shambas (homesteads with wattle and daub, thatched, windowless little rectangular houses among the banana trees) they seemed to be leaning about contemplating some prohibitively difficult action. Here and there we noticed more substantial brick and tiled-roof bungalows with wooden shutters instead of windows. A surprising number had well-kept cars outside their houses, the reward for growing cotton or coffee, no doubt. One woman was energetically and rhythmically pounding something in a hollowed-out tree trunk, standing up to do it and using with both hands a stout, trimmed branch as pestle. Perhaps the others were reflecting morosely on the paradox of having to live in a paradise that was boringly flat and distressingly untidy. Nothing bracing and firm about all these acres of banana trees, they seemed to be thinking, just these great, broad leaves flapping about listlessly in all directions: the divine landscape gardener forgot about our morale when he created this lot (or however something like that translates into Luganda).

The women, dressed in long, brightly-coloured cottons, some with bustles over their already majestic proportions, looked more impressive than the men. Beside them their menfolk stood small and scraggy, their appearance in no way improved by their dress, the kanzu, a long cotton robe. Most of these nightshirt-like garments, once white, were now stained a grubby, reddish-brown by the soil. No sign here of the blood-drinking, splendidly naked, six-foot warriors of the Karamojong up in the north-east, engaged in their permanent cattle-raiding war with the Suk, equally naked but shorter and more cunning, each tribe so murderously handy with its eight-foot spears that travel among them was prohibited save by special permit. Nothing so far to match the magnificent physique of West African men, or of the Sudanese.

As we approached Kampala, a multi-coloured city built at about 4,000 feet on several flat-topped hills, the landscape did at last become less monotonous. With a background of modern buildings painted pink, ochre or white, among many greens instead of mainly banana, the people in the town and nearby looked more varied and considerably more animated. Tall, stately Nubian women with gold in their noses stood out above the Baganda (the people of the Kingdom of Buganda, the southern part of Uganda, with its seat of government at Kampala, on Mengo Hill). The Nubian men looked professionally military, and all the taller for their fezzes. These were descendants of several hundred soldiers enlisted, with their families, by Lugard (see biographical index) in the service of the Imperial British East Africa Company in 1891. They had been led down from Southern Sudan by Selim Bey, one of Emin Pasha's commanders, after the latter, encircled by the Mahdists, had reluctantly allowed himself to be "rescued" by Stanley and had left most of his army behind. After serving Lugard, some of these Sudanese soldiers had settled in Kampala: their progeny now added greatly to the variety of its street scene. We saw Hindu women walking out in the beautiful colours of their silk saris. Parsees and Goans wore European frocks, Pakistanis their tunics with pantaloons. Purposeful, hairily-bearded Sikhs in turbans drove about fiercely. Splendidly dressed, sturdy Baganda women strolled along a few paces behind their sometimes ragged men, or kneeled submissively in the dust when addressed by them, or rode side-saddle and smiling on the carrier of a puny husband's bicycle as he pedalled laboriously home from shopping. These women's clothes fitted because all had been made for them, nothing bought from a rack. We even saw one or two whites.

Now, with some surprise, we learned that simply by coming to East Africa we had suddenly changed from "British" to "European". No matter what we thought, in everyone else's eyes we had taken our place in our particular category among the three into which the whole population was legally divided: Africans, Asians and Europeans. Racial status determined, among other things, the sort of property one could own: African land-ownership was protected. One might have been born and have grown up in Kampala or Mombasa or Dar-es-Salaam, yet it was one's parentage and colour that determined one's status as, for example, "Asian" (that is, from India or of Indian descent, or from Pakistan). A "European" might have come from America or South Africa. Some "Europeans" were actually Europeans in the terminology of the fifties, from Switzerland or Sweden, or from Italy. The latter, mainly road-builders, performed other services too. An African woman once told us that her daughter had been fathered by an Italian roadworker and that conceiving her had been by far the best time she had ever had. There was in Kampala even one exceptional woman from Vienna, but more about her later. Most "Europeans", however, were British.

Such legal categories gave a misleading impression of unity within each. Although it was accurate to describe the resident population of Kampala as predominantly "Asian", Sikhs consorted with Ismaelis not at all, while Hindus shunned the society of each of them. Goans kept to themselves. As we shall see, "Africans" around Kampala remained as distinct in their various tribes, each regarding the others as foreign.

Soon we arrived at Makerere Hill itself, just within the municipal boundary. On our right we passed the tiny, tree-shaded, plain white mosque as we took the main road up to the summit. There, along the ridge, ran the College's imposing central building, massed with colonial symmetry on either side of its clock tower. This substantial headquarters contained capacious offices, lecture rooms, and a large hall for ceremonies, plays or concerts. At each end of it, but distinct, stood externally identical chapels, Catholic and Protestant, tactfully asserting an equal self-importance at this elevated centre of the campus. As though to keep didactic grandeur within limits, in the hushed heat of the afternoon a ragged African stood resting by the road in the shade of a telephone pole. Nearly at the bottom of the slope we saw the newest residence, Northcote Hall, forbiddingly long and prison-like. Off on different sides, we were told, stood laboratories, School of Art, workshops. Across the valley, Mulago Hill with its extensive teaching hospital and new laboratories, a great institution for tropical medicine that had started in 1913 as a small dispensary for treating venereal disease. This was the hospital for Africans and Asians: for Europeans there was a small one in Kampala.

On Makerere, falling away from the summit were spacious lawns, not fine English grass but coarse, broad-leafed, more resistant to heat. A recently acquired powered gang-mower kept them trim: here and there, in the older way, lines of African labourers in tattered, tucked-up "kanzus" rhythmically swung sharpened metal strips. Along lower roads, houses sheltered persons as yet unknown. Most had to be gardeners, for roses, frangipani, orange day lilies, sisal, mulberry, poinsettia, canna lilies, plumbago, bougainvillaea, jasmine, bamboo and avocado all flourished behind exuberantly flowering hedges of yellow cassia or red and cream hibiscus. Dense groups of mango trees huddled stolidly here and there in the open spaces. Up on the ridge were two great flame trees. Nearby, a solitary clump of tall eucalyptus sentinels stood guard, taciturn Australian mercenaries in blue and silver uniform, on watch for the arrival of some distant event. Was it possible after all that the earthly paradise long sought by Moslems, Christians and Orientals alike was here, a finite speck? Specific in time as well as space, if so, for around the base of this idyllic hill we could see rebellious ranks of elephant grass (pennisetum purpureum, as we later learned) standing there in masses ten feet high as though awaiting their chance to march back and re-occupy the clearings. Just into these thickets were African semi-urban villages, their life soon to be revealed to us. That first night, despite fatigue from the journey, we slept little. Drumming and shouting from the nearest village went on until dawn. Cicadas in the cassia avenue outside our windows kept up a stupefying volume of dissonant screeching. Next day I was to begin my supposedly serious tasks!

The new house to be built for us had hardly been started; we were put up in a small flat in the new Hall of Residence. Despite all the good efforts made by Mr Tomusange, the warden's clerk, and by the European domestic bursar, herself sick with frequently recurring migraines, in a couple of days we three hapless newcomers, our resistance to Oxfordshire's bugs now irrelevant, all went down with dysentery. Fortunately it was bacillary, not the amoebic sort. Weakly, through the stench of disgusting symptoms that seemed to presage a Dantean Inferno, we contemplated what we were sure was our lack of a future. With recovery, reprieve, our initiation into Paradiso continued. Mr Tomusange proved a friendly, informed guide, far more capable than his job required. A thin Muganda of medium height, bright and birdlike, he switched rapidly back and forth between solemnity and lively humour. His English he peppered liberally with the "i" tacked on to the end of words in East African fashion: "daktari" for doctor, "kabadi" for cupboard.

What to wear in our new life? For women it was easy: the simpler styles of summer frocks brought from England, or copied in Kampala in Swiss cottons, or home-made from patterns. On the Hill we found an absorbed interest in the comparative merits of various sewing machines. One lecturer in agricultural economics proved expert at running up underwear on his Necchi. When demand was slack he turned his hand to sewing covers for his car seats. For men too, it turned out, the answer was straightforward. In 1953 the standard of daytime dress for Europeans held not only on the Hill but also in the commercial offices in Kampala or at the Protectorate Government's headquarters at Entebbe, or out in the offices of District

Commissioners and suchlike. It was a satisfyingly simple standard, cool and misleadingly egalitarian. Whether or not it suited the complexion, khaki was *de rigueur*. One went into Kampala to be measured by an Asian tailor who next day brought forth a suitable supply of well-made, easily washable, cotton shorts and open-necked, short-sleeved shirts with two pockets on the chest. Stockings showed off the manly vigour of one's calves. This was without doubt a most sensible and convenient rig given that in those days nobody seemed to have heard about skin cancer. Almost all men went hatless. Only in Zanzibar, later, was I advised to wear a panama. In six years I saw one sun-helmet on a European (some elderly Africans wore handed-down ones) and that was on the head of Carey Francis, the headmaster who was to be my host in Kenya when I first ventured into Mau-Mau country.

One or two Europeans on the Hill, medical men, went so far as to flout convention by sporting a white version of the standard rig, while the professor of education alone went about in a lightweight suit, for reasons never revealed. In all innocence and ignorance, however, others exposed much, as we were soon warned by the older women on the Hill, some precisely outspoken about their observation of male anatomy. Current fashion required both trousers and shorts to be cut very full. This was, and is still, commendable in trousers but although pleasantly cool in shorts it frequently had disconcerting consequences. American shorts fitted snugly around the thigh. Ours, on the contrary, stood out amply, a condition accentuated by the thick khaki cotton. Sitting down, therefore, caused one's shorts not only to ride up a little but to open up at the legs as well. Given the relaxing heat, given too that most men's underwear was loose and flimsy, it becomes easy to understand how one might regret that men had not been brought up to use women's tricks of modesty. Often we were astonished at the insouciance with which even the most proper would be unaware of how much they were revealing. In case such fashions ever come back, a caution may be acceptable. Crossing the legs in no way guarantees immunity.

Whether it was fundamentally this absorbing feature of tropical life or subtle compensatory social changes towards greater formality as imperial confidence ebbed, in a year or two shorts were giving way to khaki longs. By the time we left East Africa, lightweight suits had started to replace even the informal trousers. For whatever reason, senior members of government felt unable to persist in their egalitarian khaki disguise; their example had begun to filter down. They might have

9

been thought to be catching up with Africans, for the handful of African members of academic staff on the Hill, Joseph Lule and others, had never conformed to the earlier fashion. From the start of our time there they had preferred suits, or at least long trousers and shirtsleeves in the heat of the day. The students too, almost entirely African (I remember only two Asians and two Europeans), chose longs. Presumably they assumed this greater formality as distinguishing them from the short-trousered mission schoolboys they had been until recently, and as marking their aspiration to earn University of London degrees. Thus while they put off their school uniform on coming to Makerere, we European newcomers, in our earlier days, adopted it. African students had an acute sense of the bizarre and absurd. They found it wonderfully amusing to see a tall and burly Makerere adminis-trator striding about energetically, balding on top but sprouting gingerish hair exuberantly between his schoolboy shorts and stockings.

Women students all wore European frocks. Such modern young women rejected the standard Buganda busuti (derived from "bustle", we were told), a long, wrap-around, short-sleeved dress patterned on the costume of Victorian missionaries' wives, but shorts they found positively unthinkable. In fact, when a new faculty wife tottered into Kampala one day wearing the very highest of heels and, for those days, excessively brief pink shorts that she took to be fashionable in the tropics, the College received vigorous protests. For to the Baganda the truth of another Victorian inheritance had become self-evident, that while it had to be accepted that a woman might strip off down to the waist if she became hot while working on the shamba, legs, or at the very least thighs, must remain demurely covered. The colour of East African skin revealed or concealed was rarely Congo black. Nubian immigrants and tribes from northern Uganda were very dark. The African peoples in general, however, were various shades, from the quite dark Baganda (some described them as blue-black) to mezzo (for example Kikuyu students from Kenya), from the copper-coloured Hamitic-Bantu herdsmen of western Uganda to the light coffee of some born on the slopes of Kilimanjaro. "Black" is a poor description of such beautiful variation. Even "brown", suitably qualified, ignores the suggestions of green or magenta in the depths of East African skin. While driving north one day, many miles from Kampala, I passed a woman standing up in a washtub taking a bath in front of her house. She turned away from me modestly, so that what I saw for an instant was her copper-coloured back, with its wet highlights like those in the best quality orange pekoe tea. In our first few days in Uganda, however, our concerns were necessarily more practical than aesthetic. Pressing domestic problems crowded in.

Chapter 2   Learning Fast

Baruas at Breakfast

The question of servants awaited us on our first morning. We had been
warned the evening before that we should be expected to engage some
immediately: expected not by Europeans, so it went, but by Africans,
for we should be providing a social service. At first we thought this
transparent insincerity. We were wrong. To understand why requires a
leap of imagination, one that mirrors our own sudden discovery of the
sort of Africa we had dropped into, a world away from the traditional
tribal societies we had expected.

Like other East African towns of any size, Kampala and its modernity
had attracted a great number of Africans, mostly uneducated. Rickety
buses overloaded with bicycles, bundles and people arrived daily.
Women as well as men had left their shambas or grazing lands, many of
them distant, had cut themselves loose from tribe, clan and family to
look for work or some other sort of living. Every morning and evening
crowds walked or cycled to or from jobs in Kampala, for most of these
newcomers lived on the fringes of the town. If things became too hard
they could always try to get back to their own land and submit again to
tribal constraints. For many, however, "hard" would have to be "desperate" for that to happen. Women in particular valued their liberation
from the age-old drudgery of cultivation, their "digging" as they used to
put it. In any case, not all such Africans had rights to tribal land.
Traditional methods of cultivation and herding, persisted in despite dis-
astrous overstocking and erosion, had proved unable to feed a growing

12

population. Under the British peace, the time-honoured expedient of simply settling elsewhere was no longer permissible if it meant, as it frequently had in the past, fighting other tribes to do so. Men who in fact still had tribal rights to land had often moved away in the hope of earning money to meet their taxes. Wives and children left at home preserved their claim by cultivating and fending for themselves, which was little different from what they would have been doing anyway. Women who had come to the towns to get away from unsatisfactory marriages more often than not had left children behind with grand-mothers as an insurance against their own old age. In their new zones of sexual free-for-all around the towns, however, they found themselves having to compete with younger, unattached women.

Clearly, the strict customary rules and practices of the many distinct tribal societies could apply only confusedly and fragmentarily, if at all, to the new mixture of urban Africans. People from 40 tribes were counted in one village on the fringe of Kampala. Life for these immi-grants was exciting but unsettled, precarious yet preferable to what they had left. The Baganda, reputedly corrupt and widely regarded as conceited, a reputation not of course universally deserved, conde-scendingly regarded them as foreigners whom they had to civilise. By far the largest tribe in Uganda, the Baganda were also the best-off in terms of their soil and climate, their economy, the extent and level of their education and their favoured position in the protectorate's constitution. Moreover, other tribes had received less attention from missionaries than they: some at Makerere told us that it was this ambiguous benefit that made the Baganda apparently so pleased with themselves despite living in a sort of moral no-man's-land between their profession of belief and the life of civic and private virtue as defined, by no means unanimously, by the missions. Whatever the truth of that assertion, it was undeniable that the Baganda left the African newcomers, those "barbaric inferiors", no choice but to approach civilisation by crowding into the urbanised slum villages of greater Kampala.

There these unfortunates, on the move into modernity, found no established form of marriage. Christian or Moslem standards, accepted by a small minority (and then only partially), jostled with the confusion of customary practices. They all failed to stem the slide into promiscuity in various forms, from outright prostitution for food or money to the kaleidoscopic patterns of lovers with multiple partners. Here and there more stable informal unions stood out. These might last a few months, possibly a year or two. As one African woman put it to a researcher, "After all, men as well as women (here) are like plates used in a hotel. Anyone is free to use them." Among the many consequences of this shift to a new life, the most obvious were poverty and crime. Some of the immigrants managed to do moderately well by starting small enterprises such as trading, butchering, water-carrying, or by selling beer brewed from bananas, maize, millet or pineapples, or by distilling and selling the illegal waragi, also known as Nubian gin. Many more were hard put to it to pay the rent and buy enough to eat. Hence the abundance of thieves in the fringe villages. Women and small children could be seen stealing from the lorries that lurched in with plantains, burglars broke into flimsy houses, self-ingratiating drinkers stayed alert in order to rob drunks. Among both men and women drunkenness and brawling were common. Fights could hardly be avoided, given the mixture of drinking with the prevalent promiscuity, for while marital stability was almost entirely absent, jealousy and sexual aggression were rife. This was a scene whose wild and desperate vitality Hogarth or Dickens would have recognised. As for venereal disease, one African woman put it succinctly: "Not only Africans, but everyone has it," meaning Asian and European men too, some of whom kept mistresses in the fringe or picked up African women there in bars. Accompanying all these problems there were the pressing ones of homelessness, unemployment and malnutrition.

The listless people we had seen beside the road from Entebbe, even these fortunate landowners, were malnourished. Their diet consisted too heavily of the plantains flourishing around them in such despondent confusion. These, wrapped in their leaves and steamed, were the Buganda staple. If coated with a groundnut sauce or, less often, with a little meat, they yielded more energy. Too frequently, however, it was banana (matoke) cooked alone (and expertly eaten with the index and second fingers of one hand). Other tribes, especially those from the west or the Northern Province of Uganda, relied on more nourishing staples (millet, sorghum or corn to make "posho", a sort of porridge) as well as peas, beans or lentils, so tended to be in much better condition. Most of the men in the East African regiment, the King's African Rifles, were from the north, as were the police. Yet wherever they had come from, and whether landless at home or not, once in Kampala the immigrants were cut off from food of any sort unless they could earn, beg, steal, or trust in a marginally more fortunate relative or friend. As for accommodation, in the semi-urban villages around Kampala it was hard to find a room. Mr Tomusange told me he was a lucky man: he had two. Many were forced to sleep on the floor with several others in one of the rows of such rooms put up for immigrants from other tribes by upper-class Baganda, who nevertheless in public deplored the existence of these very slums from which they profited.

No building standards governed such construction. These urban villages were in Buganda territory, its separate jurisdiction jealously guarded by the Baganda. Here the well-run modern Kampala munici-pality had no control, and even the Protectorate Government was powerless to move without endless political suspicion and compli-cations. No common services existed or were contemplated in these settlements. Unmaintained, eroded tracks served as roads, insanitary carriers sold cans of water, there was no drainage, and the pit latrines had to be shared by many households. When it rained, roofs leaked. Mud houses would sometimes wash away downhill in a storm. Pressure on accommodation was even greater in Nairobi's African slums, the perfect setting for Mau-Mau's passive army and supply channels. There it was a question not of looking for a room but of paying exorbitantly for a bed-space, not to be understood as including a bed, in an already grossly overcrowded and stinking hovel.

Fear of the powers of witchcraft added deep layers of terror to Africans' lives, whether in the tribes or in towns. In the urban villages around Kampala, for example, Africans setting themselves up in some small business would seek magical aid as a guarantee of prosperity. A magician would supply for a large fee a small dried plant to be hung in the shop, there to exert its power to transfer other people's wealth to the new proprietor. If success proved elusive, as it usually did, Africans would blame somebody else's counter-witchcraft. A competitor must have smoked a pipe of magical herbs at midnight, then thrown the pipe on the steps of whichever shop he wanted to fail.

A murder trial that arose from the death of an African woman in Uganda in 1957 brought to light the techniques in the countryside of a widely-feared witch-doctor, Kimote Muwanga. This man had killed his mistress during a quarrel after they had been drinking together. Having dumped the body in the bush he set about defending himself at once with his magic. First he offered coffee berries and coins to the deceased's ghost to placate it. Then, using urine and blood, he pronounced spells to divert suspicion from himself to a tree root, a discarded piece of banana tree, and a splinter of dried wood. When finally summoned by his chief to come for questioning by the police, he made a clay image of himself and kneaded into it his own finger and toe-nail clippings, with hairs from his head. He had an assistant build a little beehive hut for it in the bush and shut it up there, the point being to divert suspicion from himself on to the image. This was all to no avail, in spite of his local power, for the assistant, not of the brightest, revealed everything. Muwanga was found guilty of manslaughter and sentenced to 10 years. Throughout East Africa it was not only the sorcery of other Africans that the various tribes feared. They were convinced beyond all power of rational argument that Europeans too practised their own incomprehensible magic, sometimes beneficent but at other times horrifyingly malign.

With his effective mixture of deference and firmness, Mr Tomusange told us at our first breakfast, when I was looking forward to getting to know some of the students, that we had to come out and deal with a long line of applicants for our domestic jobs. There they stood by the cassia avenue, stood and waited, men and women of various ages, some of the women clean, alert, and brightly dressed, some of the men in filthy rags, several looking ill. We asked Mr Tomusange to announce that until our house was built, or until we moved temporarily into another, we had no need of and unfortunately no housing for more than an ayah (nursemaid). This he did at some length. Nobody moved or spoke. He explained to us that each one of them badly needed a job and somewhere to live. This impasse we had neither the language nor other means to resolve. Everyone in the line held a piece of paper (or "barua") in his hand. These were references from previous employers. As we were to discover later, they were not always complimentary: "Steer clear of this rogue" one of them read, and another, "Give this man a wide berth". Never, we had been warned, employ anyone who has no barua. Yet the resulting brisk trade in these documents was well known: frequently they were borrowed or stolen. Faced with all these complications and conflicting pulls on our sympathies, we asked Mr Tomusange to select an ayah for us. To his credit, he chose not from his own tribe, as might have been expected, but a handsome young Mutoro, Mary, from far away in south-western Uganda. He examined her barua carefully, questioned her, and negotiated terms between us. When we had agreed to take each other on he explained to the rest, or so we took him to be saying, that the only job available had now gone. As before, nobody moved or spoke. All we could do was withdraw with Mary. Some hours later there were still a few standing in line. The domestic bursar gave them a meal before they eventually left.

When we moved out of the hall into a temporary house, Mary came with us and we added a gardener (that is, in what was the accepted language, a shamba-boy, no matter what the person's age) and a cook-houseboy. These were all we had room for. The house was small; up in the garden stood only three of the one-room, thatched huts for servants. Our new house, however, was built surprisingly fast by a Sikh contractor especially engaged by the college; he employed both Sikhs and Africans as his fundis (skilled workmen, more or less). With it came a row of four concrete, tiled-roof, unfurnished rooms with a communal lavatory and washroom at one end. The row was connected to the house by walls that formed a compound with its own door to the outside. We looked out on it from our kitchen door and windows and enjoyed the feeling of mutual familial responsibility, as we all lived closely but not intimately together. One day we saw that our staff had planted a row of corn in the compound's beaten red earth. Given our sympathies with the long struggle in Britain to do away with slums, our initial shame at having to offer such basic accommodation was understandable. Yet it was inappropriate in our new situation. These quarters, concrete-floored, clean, private, and with running water, our staff considered preferable to the older huts on the Hill and superior by a very long way to anything they could hope to afford to rent in or near Kampala. They were safer, too, for we listened with horrified fascination to Peter Gutkind's tales about Mulago village. Always affably and volubly ready to talk about his researches, or of Aidan Southall's in the Kisenyi slum (these two were colleagues at the East African Institute of Social Research), he told us of the jealous suspicion and open aggression, even hatred, among African men there, of fights, of thieves caught and beaten, of a Buganda administration incapable of keeping order. One of his stories, surrealistically bizarre, seemed particularly to catch the flavour of the life our staff might have been living. An African school-teacher in Mulago had noted in his diary that early one morning he had found a human arm just "lying about". Nobody knew whose it was or how it had come there. Possibly it had been slashed from a thief, for people had heard shouting during the night (not in itself unusual) but if so, where was the rest of him? Perhaps a hungry dog had run off with it from the hospital? Yet how odd for a starving creature to leave it there ungnawed after going to the trouble of carrying it away. It had been late in the evening before the Buganda police had got around to taking it off in a van.

We promoted the cook-houseboy to cook and engaged a houseboy to occupy the fourth room. At first our servants tended to move on fairly soon. Mary went home to Toro after a year. Before she left, we discovered a theft and Mr Tomusange came to the house to question the staff. Under pressure, Mary told him that "Memsahib didn't know what she had". Reported to us, this remark led us to wonder if she would have volunteered it. Uneasily, we checked the contents of our various drawers, cupboards and boxes. One large trunk that we used as a chest we found to be empty of a generous quantity of our linen sheets and pillowcases that it was supposed to be protecting. In our trusting innocence we had scorned locking it. Who had taken them we never knew for certain. Africans, accustomed to sharing property among relations, nevertheless recognised the difference between such accepted sharing and theft.

It was at about this time that our household began to settle down into the shape it was to maintain for the rest of our time in East Africa. Two remarkable women came to us. Alisi was a Moslem Muganda whose husband had knocked her about and was now in prison. When we engaged her she was in her twenties, round-faced, fairly short and plump, shy, frightened even, round-eyed and very solemn. As she settled down, her cheerfulness came out. Sensitive, delicate, she was also intelligent and active. Her quiet "Bado kidogo" ("In a little while") was not the common procrastination but to say that she had an orderly plan. Her occasional "Kasi mingi" ("What a lot of work!") was not a complaint or excuse but a fair assessment. Often she had long conversations with my wife. They arose out of trivial events but would expand into thoughtful discussions. Particularly knowledgeable about human nature, she judged people shrewdly and interpreted their gestures minutely. For Africans, gestures were full of meaning and well understood. Europeans put too much emphasis on words, Alisi thought, too little on gestures and facial expression. When we told her something that surprised her she would exclaim with a sharp "Eh" of indrawn breath. Soon she had become our cook-housekeeper, an unusual but mutually happy arrangement: cooks were supposed to be men. Nothing was lost from our house once Alisi and Nyesi came to it. From the same western tribe as Mary, Nyesi was a mature, solidly built, middle-aged woman who had kicked out her ne'er-do-well husband. As an ayah she was unsurpassed on the Hill. Whenever we were out for the evening she would bring in her mat and sleep on the threshold of our son's room. Anyone who might have tried to get past would have encountered a stout peasant arm. That would have been an experience not to be taken lightly, for across the valley, in Mulago village, an independent African woman had recently demonstrated her strength by beating a man almost senseless for calling her a prostitute. Nyesi was unfailingly sensible and reliable.

What we liked most about Alisi and Nyesi (who got on well without, apparently, being intimate friends) was their confidence in themselves: not their style to fawn and flatter. One day Alisi needed to go home to her shamba to see her mother on some family business. I drove her the 50 or so miles from Kampala, soon off the metalled road and along tracks deep into the bananas. Eventually we arrived at Alisi's land and pulled up in a clearing with several small, thatched, wattle-and-daub, windowless houses around it. I was introduced to her mother, who curtsied low and stayed down in the traditional manner of the Baganda; I was expected to return her greetings and ask her to get up. Then I waited while they went indoors to complete whatever their business was. When they came out, after a brief murmured consultation they shyly beckoned me towards the smallest of the houses and led me inside. There, standing in the almost-dark, in a hut virtually empty save for the low, leather-thonged wooden bed, was Alisi's grandmother. Tiny, spare, wizened, bent, and looking unbelievably aged, she greeted me by taking my hand affectionately between hers and smiling up at me with an exquisite youthfully bright contentment. Evidently the three of them managed very well on their own land and with Alisi's earnings, without Alisi's husband or, apparently, any other man. Probably they employed a labourer from Ruanda-Urundi occasionally to harvest the cotton. It seemed to me not at all likely that this grandmother would have to be left out to die because they could not feed her. When we said goodbye, they gave me a small package of eggs wrapped in banana leaves and tied with a strip of rag, to take home to my wife. On the way back to Makerere, Alisi had an even more than usually self-contained presence. She looked what she was, a prudent woman of property, a beneficiary of the fact that the British had introduced the system of land ownership that permitted African women to inherit and own land.

Although we never met Alisi's husband, one of us did meet Nyesi's: in a sense, that is. Once when I was on safari, my wife heard a hulla-baloo at the back of the house in the middle of the night. Alisi and Nyesi were shouting, a most unusual thing. She unlocked the kitchen door and looked out, only to be turned on by a strange African who was out there furiously trying to set fire to a pile of clothes and bedclothes (Nyesi's, as it turned out), with the two women and our other staff trying to restrain him. He turned drunkenly on my wife and shouted at her in Kitchen Swahili, "Go back to your hut, woman!" Alisi and Nyesi explained rapidly that this was Nyesi's husband who, having arrived drunk and unannounced in the hope of persuading her to take him back, was now retaliating with amorous arson for her vigorous refusal. They entreated "Memsahib" to go indoors since he was "a badi man": they would deal with him. This she sensibly did, leaving them to it. Too much drink, fortunately, reduces amorous powers however expressed. The two women turned him around three times and packed him off into his drunken night. He was not heard of again while we were there.

Helping Alisi and Nyesi on that occasion were the other two in our quartet. Abunwazi, our houseboy, was young, not very bright, clumsy, friendly and willing. Alisi kept him in order and told him what to do. A hilarious regular event enjoyed by all was Abunwazi's attempt to polish the red-painted concrete floors by skating all over them on sheepskin pads. The last of the four was the mysterious Jaylus, a stocky, middle-aged man who was our shamba-boy. Alisi and Nyesi would whisper that he must be a jailbird. By drinking away his wages he remained inter-mittently penniless and permanently in rags. Banana beer he regarded as his food, a view common among African immigrants in Kampala. He rarely spoke and never smiled. How we came to take him on I am not at all sure. Yet there grew up between my wife and him a successful if odd gardening arrangement. She would ask him to do whatever it was to be for that morning. He would say nothing and walk away to begin something else. Then when my wife had gone inside again he would set himself to the appointed task, working steadily but with a lowering scowl of disgust until he felt tired, when he would sit down wherever he happened to be. If he thought my wife was looking out he would reluctantly start again. By much patient and indirect encouragement on her part and his sporadic bursts of energy, between them they created in time around the new house a beautiful garden. The African under-graduates, as they told us themselves when they came to tea, regarded the result as a waste of time and labour. Cultivation, as they understood it, should be for food, not beauty. Although he had no English as far as we knew, Jaylus would stand by in his tatters scowling his agreement with these well-dressed, talkative young men. They ignored him pointedly and must have seemed as far removed from himself as we were. Not all Africans took such an exclusively utilitarian view of gardens. Here and there we used to see little plots of flowers outside African houses.

It was generally agreed that Bernard de Bunsen's servants must be a thieving lot, for at luncheon at his house there would never be enough food, not even boiled potatoes, let alone meat. One had to plan on eating at home afterwards. Other things of his were at risk, too. One night he returned late from dining out to find that all his clothes had been taken, down to his pyjamas and last sock. The thieves had left him with what he was wearing, his dinner jacket, so that for a meeting in his office at 8.00am next day, before he could get into Kampala to re-stock, he was forced to appear somewhat overdressed. It was the mystery of Bernard's sugar, however, that intrigued us all. His chief houseboy, a taciturn man with polished manners, was said to steal it. As Bernard would tell us himself with wry humour, he used to puzzle over his grocer's bills and ask himself with unworldly wonder how he could possibly be consuming so much sugar. He made a new year's resolution to give up taking it in his coffee, or so it was reported. By the time we left Makerere, Bernard's bachelor household's sugar consumption, according to the stories circulating at dinner parties, was prodigious.

On the Hill it was acknowledged that African servants would steal from time to time. It would have been surprising had they not. As everyone knew, theft of food and equipment from Mulago Hospital went on constantly. Nevertheless, when we bought our refrigerator in Kampala we were embarrassed to find that it came with a lock and key. Never before had we seen or imagined such a thing. In East Africa, all refrigerators were lockable. Fortunately we had no need to lock ours as soon as Alisi and Nyesi were in charge. In any case, as most of our colleagues did, we distributed tea and sugar to our staff as well as a supplement to wages for kuni (firewood). That seemed the best way to reduce temptations. At dinner parties we were among those who had stories to tell instead of making the standard complaints about servants that surfaced occasionally. Here is one of my wife's tales as she told it after dinner over the coffee and chocolate mints.

Hue and Cry

"I was in the house one afternoon and heard a great noise of people hurrying past, most unusual in the heat of the day. When I looked out, there was a crowd of Africans streaming through the garden and into the elephant grass, all ululating and very excited. Staff in their grubby singlets and ragged shorts came rushing out from Northcote Hall kitchens to catch up with the leaders. They too ran past, ululating shrilly like the others, and disappeared into the grass in the direction of the "pombe" (banana beer) shop that's a short way in there. I had not the least idea what was going on, but soon the crowd returned. Nyesi, I was astonished to see, was leading it. With her came our ragged old shamba-boy, Jaylus. He had no choice in the matter: she had him by the scruff of the neck and kneed him in the back whenever he slowed! Nyesi pointed to the house with her chin, African fashion, and shouted: 'Call the police, memsahib, while I hold this thief!'

"Without thinking, I telephoned at once to the Protectorate Police, not the Kabaka's. (The Kabaka was the King of Buganda. In fact, His Highness's police force, poorly trained and corrupt, was spurned even by his own chiefs in cases of crime: they too preferred to go to the protectorate force.)

"We had only a few minutes to wait before a tall African askari (constable), very black, from a northern tribe as most of the police are, came marching up the Hill. He was imposingly smart in his well-pressed khaki uniform, with shorts, black puttees and belt, polished boots, and wearing his black fez with its tassel and police badge on the front. He came equipped with his truncheon, handcuffs and an excited grin. His first words, in English, were, 'Where is the criminal? I want to arrest the criminal.'

"This pleased the equally excited crowd greatly. Here was a grand Protectorate Policeman: this was an occasion. Nyesi then said she had seen Jaylus take her gold wristwatch from her room and make off with it for the pombe shop. She had raised the hue and cry and set out after him. Jaylus, plainly tipsy, had been protesting while she spoke. Now he muttered an insult to which the askari replied by hitting him sharply on the head with his truncheon. Jaylus's nose bled and out from his mouth popped a ten shilling note. The crowd roared with delight, for they thought it was obvious how Jaylus had come by the money. The askari, of like mind, pocketed the note as evidence, snapped the handcuffs on

22

him, and to everyone's great satisfaction marched him off to be charged and held in the protectorate gaol. Had the askari not been there, of course, the crowd would have beaten Jaylus severely as a thief. Across the valley, in Mulago village, that happens all the time.

"When the case came up I drove in with Nyesi to the magnificent courtroom, with its imposing mahogany dock and bench. The magistrate was a youngish, worried European, soberly dressed in suit and tie. Nyesi was not called to give evidence because Jaylus pleaded guilty. Then he added, pointing with his chin to another disreputable-looking African in the court, 'He was there too'.

"This other man had certainly not been there when Nyesi caught Jaylus. He and Jaylus simply wanted a holiday together in the protectorate gaol, far more comfortable than the Kabaka's prison. You get no food from the Kabaka. If your relatives don't bring you meals, you'll starve up there. But the protectorate prisoners live in style at public expense. The Kabaka keeps his crowded and filthy.

"The magistrate called up this other man, who said yes, he was guilty too. As a District Officer in Tanganyika said once of African attitudes to such court proceedings, 'Any lie is good enough to deceive a European'. Before sentencing, it was revealed that Jaylus was an habitual offender. He had been in and out of native prisons for years, but this was the first time he had reached the distinction of appearing before a protectorate court. Neither Jaylus nor his friend had money to pay the fine so each received the sentence he was hoping for. Now, to judge by Jaylus's expression as the askaris led the two rogues off, he was looking forward to a rest from gardening.

"Nyesi definitely feels vindicated by having Jaylus sent to gaol. Her prized watch, however, she has never seen again. Our new shamba-boy is Joseph, much duller but rather more reliable."

Chapter 3   Moonflowers and Chameleons

On Makerere Hill, that concentrated, idyllic little garden enclave under the equatorial sun, various distractions had their disadvantages. Our overseas editions of *The Times* and *TLS* used to arrive unpredictably, and tended to look daunting as they piled up unread. Local newspapers, the *East African Standard* and *Uganda Argus*, while occasionally interesting, had after a while a stultifying, provincial tone. Although the Uganda Society's *Uganda Journal* was never dull, with its articles on many aspects of life in the protectorate, it appeared only twice a year. There was the unfailing pleasure of serious reading, especially of things deferred until such an opportunity as this, and study, but like most people we needed the relaxation of a relapse into triviality now and again. Out there, under what we soon came to feel was the melancholy sameness of tropical sunshine, we could not even fall back on British small-talk about the weather and its seasons; or allow ourselves, on the other hand, to linger debilitatingly over home thoughts.

"Can you afford," a colleague asked me one day from behind his most charmingly serious smile, "to miss another spring?"

Such nostalgic seductions were best avoided, yet some Europeans were determined to pine their lives away. Fortunately, then, there was one absorbing distraction on the Hill that cut across all others. Housing, provided by the college, and always near the heart of everyone's domestic interest, was a limitless subject of gossip that brought out the full nobility of expatriate emotion, from envy through covetousness to pride and contempt. There were other, more subtle, distinctions that it generated, for example between those who preferred the older, colonial houses and those who sought the grander, solid, modern style. It was among the latter group that the most vicious, backbiting competition occurred. Happily for those who enjoyed this game, it could be played by long-established, juvenile rules. Bigger was better. Bigger was also, in fact, higher up the Hill until, wondrous achievement to attain one of them, there on the highest point of the ridge stood two minor mansions worthy of Wimbledon and distinguished from almost all other housing on the Hill by not being bungalows. Thus they were all the more prestigious in the aspiring eyes of climbers, who stared with naked desire at the upstairs bedroom windows.

Quite low on the Hill cringed the lowest, a block of small flats down near Wandegeya market. Their flimsy construction cunningly ensured that everything that took place in any one of them could be heard clearly in the next. A young lecturer swore against all sceptics that he could hear the woman next door brushing her hair. Another resident, a spinster, delighted everyone with a memorable slip of the tongue worthy of Spooner himself. She said of her neighbours, a couple married but a few weeks before, that she could hear their houseboy knock to bring in their early morning tea, and then she could hear "the rats coupling".

One step above these flats in the hierarchy of housing were some wooden bungalows built on struts on the other, steeper, side of the Hill. Particularly hot in the evening, their rooms were narrow. They suffered above all from having about them a feeling of insecurity, as though termites were waiting their chance to chew through the last fibres of a strut or two and send the whole cottage, sweating occupants with it, tumbling over and over down the steep slope and into the blue evening haze of waving banana leaves below.

Midway in altitude and prestige among the new housing, on the moderate slope facing Mulago Hill and its hospital, were the brick and roughcast bungalows built along new winding lanes. Like the ultimates on the crest, they had Bangalore tiled roofs (the full significance of which will become clear shortly) and, as everywhere on Makerere, they were immersed in the abundant greenery of their gardens. One moonlit night, when walking arm-in-arm back from dining at one of these houses, we were stopped a few doors away by a pool of heavy voluptuous fragrance. Just above us, beginning its climb up the lamp standard, we saw for the first time the aptly named calonyction (nightly-blooming beauty), its hand-sized, generous, pure white, odoriferous trumpets pouring their sweet siren-call into the still air. By morning nothing would remain of this seductive scent of moonflowers[1]. Even as we waded out of its spell its traces turned up a pungent, slightly sinister edge towards the rank, pervasive smell of termites. Frequently during our six years on the Hill our evening walk took us in search of that haunting garden scent. Usually we were too early for it.

Although palatial compared with some of the Public Works Department housing for colonial officers and their families in the field elsewhere in East Africa, and no matter how consoling their greenery, their occupants felt these middling houses on the Hill to be cramped both inside and out. Through flourishing cassia or hibiscus hedges it was all too possible to touch neighbours' washing, hear their music or altercations, be invaded by their children, and to feel, some comfortably but others emphatically not, that apart from the climate and the flora one had landed in an English suburb where the houses, on close acquaintance, failed to live up to the advertisements. Inside, an oppressive amount of space was taken up by the standard issue of settee and chairs of a design locally called "Morris". This heavy furniture in dark mahogany, well made in the college workshops, had wide arm-pieces and adjustable backs. Four-inch-thick, kapok-filled, removable cushions covered its cane seats and backs with rectangular, magenta slabs. Such furniture, eminently sensible and utilitarian, might for those reasons have been approved of by William Morris himself, even though these attenuated examples of his influence lacked the grace of his own productions. Nevertheless, combined with depressingly durable side-boards, dining tables and chairs, thick square coffee tables and, in the bedrooms, similar furniture in the same wood, it succeeded in making the inside of these bungalows look as identical as the outside, and all equally cramped.

In spite of distinctions of desirability among these dwellings, some higher up the slope and larger, nothing could overcome their dreadful

1   Moonflowers: common name for the three species that form the botanical genus Calonyction (from the Greek kalos, beautiful, and nyktos, night) of the Convolvulus family. Native to the tropics, these night-flowering climbers can reach a height of 15 feet. Their heavily fragrant, white trumpet-blooms, as much as six inches across, open in the late evening among their handsome, heart-shaped leaves. At first light they close or fade and shut off their scent, while new buds prepare for night.

sameness. On long hot afternoons, or in the unbounded sleeplessness of nights fractured by cicadas, they emphasised our common mortality, that waiting enemy of all pretensions to hierarchy. Imagine the horror, then, the chagrin of those senior members of the academic staff forced at each breakfast to contemplate the fact that the mansions on the crest were many fewer than could satisfy all those who believed they had a right to one. No amount of vigorous expostulation or impassioned or even quietly aggrieved appeal to the Principal could alter the ghastly tally of insufficiency. The only course (save for a quite separate choice to be revealed shortly) was to accept one of the better of these shamingly inferior bungalows and hope for a death among the undeserving, condescending, all-too-established occupants up there on the ridge.

Imagine, too, the consternation with which these misused unfortunates learned that a bungalow was being especially built for us. What was more, as work on it proceeded it became obvious to everyone that it was larger than any other new bungalow. Yet it was lowest of all on the Hill. People walked down to it in the cool evenings for the satisfaction of gnashing their teeth at this reversal of the natural order. Envy rustled in the common room, over the telephone, between the verdant gardens, no doubt in bedrooms too: especially there, perhaps. When we moved in everyone, it seemed, called on us, rather as though we were manning an Ideal Homes exhibit. What had they come to see? Above all, it was our much-talked-of living room. One stepped down into it and found oneself in a space large enough to take two sets of Morris furniture without crowding. Two, do you see, they would say. Then the Morris armchairs and settees were arranged (squarely, we could do nothing about that) around our large Wilton carpet. This immediately became an object of veneration. For Europeans it signified spaciousness. This word had to be pronounced in a special way on the Hill. One administrator had managed to persuade authority that he should have a house on the ridge if a vacancy occurred. Soon an occupant decided to move to South Africa; intense lobbying ensued. When the administrator's victory was announced the outcry smacked not at all of academic detachment. Ears were alert for anything the lucky couple might say that could be used against them. The administrator's wife provided much ammunition. One word in particular entered the Hill's esoteric vocabulary. Unguardedly she said that her new house was suitably spacious. This fatal word of pride she pronounced with an extraordinarily long, self-congratulatory "a". Thus our room was dubbed, with a smile, spa...a...aycious.

By Africans, we soon realised, the carpet was venerated as signifying ceremony. Our house staff would always walk around it, never on it. Students, even, were uneasy when they found themselves expected to stand on it. Our bearskin, a silver-tip American shot in Colorado by my wife's great-uncle in the twenties, now spread out at the verandah end of the room, was another object of wonder. Students as well as servants persisted in calling it a lion, and watched it cautiously. Moreover, we were among the few families on the Hill to have brought out some of our china, pictures and furniture. Two slender-legged pieces stood happily with the Morris. The main remaining icon from home was in the laundry room: our early Thor clothes-washing machine. We used it in Africa only a few times. Then it seized (gummed up with ants, we ignorantly speculated) and there was nobody in Kampala who could tell why, or how to get it going again. So there it sat, unusable but much admired by our staff. As soon as we arrived, one faculty wife had dismissed it with an unworthy quip, as though from Aristotle at his worst: "I already have a washing machine. Mine has black hands and it's going to use them."

Distinct from the muttering ranks of envy in the modern housing, those who preferred the older houses lived a quieter and, as they judged, a privileged life. Without question these old bungalows, dating back to the twenties and thirties, would have produced sniffs of disdain among estate agents in St John's Wood: in Holland Park they would have been unimaginable. No Bangalore tiles crowned these archaic dwellings. Instead, their roofs were of corrugated iron, so that whenever there was a downpour (Buganda specialises in dramatic, colossally and satisfyingly violent thunderstorms) the noise inside made conversation difficult. Their brick construction was stuccoed with what seemed to consist largely of dried mud, whitewashed. Along the base of all walls not protected by a verandah ran a yard-high ochre stain from the rain splash. Every such house had its concrete-floored verandah, some screened in with mosquito-proof metal netting, others not. Yet this difference, we realised on our evening walks, was typical of these old houses. No two had been built to quite the same plan. Not so much designed as put together to meet this need or that as it arose, they gave evidence of having been sited individually and spontaneously back in days when a shortage of space on the Hill must have seemed a prospect not worth considering. Spread out irregularly among the lawns, they kept their considerable distance from each other, successful survivors of earthquake tremors (one day, out in the garden, the ground shuddered beneath me as though an express train were roaring past close by). Their gardens varied, too. People in the past had said, "We don't want too much to keep up. This will be enough. Plant the hedge close, here," or, "If we take the hedge out as far as the anthill we can plant a second frangipani and give it room to spread. And beyond that an avocado, don't you think? They'll both mature long before we retire."

These older houses, then, had the advantages of unplanned variety, privacy, beauty of setting, and a sense of continuity with others who had come and gone. Their various occupants became deeply attached to them. Bernard de Bunsen wisely resisted all suggestions that as Principal he should move further up the crest. He stayed in his shady old-style bungalow, the Principal's residence from the days before Makerere's expansion. It was not quite as elevated as the upstart two-storey mansions but it had a marvellous view of Kampala, including the site of Lugard's fort, was much more dignified and suited his character.

We felt ourselves fortunate, after three years in our envied new bungalow, when one of these old ones fell vacant just as I was appointed Director of Extra-Mural Studies, and we were able to move in. Our nearest, distant neighbours were three bachelors: Sandy Galloway, Dean of Medicine, to enter whose elegant house, built in 1922, the first on the Hill, was like stepping back into the eighteenth century, with candles lit in the daytime; Victor Ford, a shy geographer who knew all there was to know about trade on Lake Victoria, with his allegedly fierce Alsatian, Husky; and the quiet and wise Professor of Geography, Kenneth Baker. The four households were a perfection of mutually well-disposed, congenial non-interference. We rarely saw each other but happily accepted remote signs of each other's continued existence. Typically, benevolent authority judged our new house to be inadequate for our recently increased family and built on an extra bedroom.

What we were delighted to find ourselves in was a small, asymmetrical house. Its narrow sitting room ran back from the front door to meet, at a right angle, the much narrower screened kitchen along the back. On the left of the sitting room as one came up the three front steps was the dining room. On the right, our bedroom with its verandah, not screened, and beyond that a dressing room that we used for our infant daughter Julia, the bathroom with its erratic geyser and ancient bath on feet, the added bedroom for Charles or guests, and the lavatory outside. Doors and window frames were in heavy mahogany. High rooms, shaded by verandah and trees, remained reasonably cool in spite of the iron roof. As well as screened windows that we kept open all day for the breeze, high up in the walls there were screened ventilation spaces. It was truly a tropical garden house, admirably suited to the climate.

Behind it, up the Hill a little, across a patch of grass, was the row of rooms for Alisi and the others. These were smaller than those they had had at the new bungalow but in fact, they said, they now preferred these older, leafy, very informal surroundings to the restriction and heat of their former walled compound. At night (it was dark soon after seven), after Alisi's "Kwa heri" ("Goodnight") to each of us in her gentlest voice, whenever the sitting room back door was open we could see them making their cooking fires between our kitchen and their houses. By now Alisi had changed from her overall into an old busuti, navy blue with large, dark red flowers, that she kept for relaxed times and that suited her handsome skin. As they steamed their traditional bundles of leaf-wrapped bananas and prepared their meat or groundnut sauce, they chatted and laughed, dark figures crouching bright-faced beside their fire or walking serenely back and forth, in and out of the shadows of their own flame-lit world, dignified and at home. In this beautiful and peaceful scene they and we all felt secure. Charles (Charlesi, African fashion, to them) would sneak out in his pyjamas to beg a taste of matoke and join in their chat: that must be the ideal way to learn a language. When in 1975 I saw in Toronto an exhibition of Puvis de Chavannes' idyllic visions of antiquity, it was memories of that graceful evening scene in our Makerere garden that, seemingly irrelevantly, his paintings retrieved for me.

A good place, Makerere, to bring up young children, the old hand had said before we left England. So we found it, for infants and through primary school. After that, if parents stayed, it meant boarding school in Kenya or England. From the start, that prospect limited the time we planned to spend in East Africa. We were not against boarding school, but the thought of such a great separation deterred us from thinking of a long stay. Kenya would have been nearer, of course, but in many respects it seemed too uncertain a place to justify sending our children there.

When we arrived in East Africa, Charles had reached the great age of one and a half: to Africans, a "toto". He went at once into a group of similar stalwarts, rakish in their sunhats – Martin Tenniswood, Jonty Calder, the two Beachey boys, Clare Ingham, Beth Fallers – who used to meet every weekday morning and early evening with their ayahs in the shade somewhere out on the Hill. In the shade, yes, but not in any shade. The dense shelter of mango trees, for example, had to be avoided because a certain fly that lived there was in the habit of mistaking human flesh for a mango and laying in it an egg that soon developed into a maggot. One found oneself with an unusual, localised, red, firm swelling. One squeezed it and out popped the maggot, an operation both satisfying and disgusting. Ayahs preferred to seek shade elsewhere, but never too near elephant grass, where the danger was different. We thoroughly approved of Africans' attitude to snakes. One or two sorts, just possibly, might be harmless, but the general principle was that all were potentially lethal.

Not long after we moved into our newly-built bungalow a snake about three feet long made the mistake of venturing into our staff's compound. Immediately they set upon it with loud cries of alarm. Beaten with sticks, stamped on, it was soon dead and thrown limply into an empty dustbin. Then Mary, our first ayah, did a dance around the compound, shuffling rhythmically, miming a limp, until finally she put her right leg into the dustbin and touched the dead snake with her heel. After a few hops, life returned to normal. Snakes, it was clear, were not to be tolerated. This had been evident just before the house was finished. We were looking over it when we heard people outside shouting and banging tins and dustbin lids. Mr Tomusange rushed in to tell us that a black mamba (an elapid, like the cobra) had been spotted by the house. As we went out, there indeed was the fearsome olive-green killer. It reared up and breasted the elephant grass that still grew a few yards away, not yet cleared for the garden. Since the grass must have been about nine feet high, this snake was no small creature. We had heard that the black mamba (from the Zulu imamba) was the largest and most feared of African venomous snakes; now we could well believe it. It forced its way into the depths: nobody cared to follow to see for himself why it was called black. Only inside its mouth is it that colour, as it displays to its terrified victim just before it strikes.

When one of our Makerere colleagues heard about it he offered to bring a selection from his extensive armoury and shoot it for us. But the mamba stayed out of sight. Not surprisingly, the ayahs would always keep well away from such dangerous places. Sitting on the short grass with their embroidery, dressed in their clean white or green overalls, they kept a close watch over their young charges, who could not in any case stray far because each was normally attached by a string to the ayah's belt. Within these genial limits they were safe. As they grew older and learned what to avoid they could roam anywhere on the Hill.

A pleasant thing about Makerere, from the children's point of view, was that there was much to interest them as they grew. Birthday parties and school yielded their trials, of course. Some parents fatuously saw even four-year-olds as already marked for a lifetime of worldly success or failure. Charles played the laggard for a while and we let him choose his own time to confound the pseudo-solicitous prophets. We did try such things as the recording of Peter and the Wolf for him to listen to: he soon found it as boring as I did. Stories after bathtime ended the evening, as for children elsewhere. There were the exotic differences, such as the reassuring forms of Nyesi or Alisi asleep on a mat in the bedroom doorway whenever we went out to dinner. Yet the main thing was that the children's life was so much more out-of-doors than would have been possible in England. Charles taught himself to swim early on in Lake Victoria, where we had gone to picnic. After that we used to take him to the Entebbe pool or to Silver Springs on the outskirts of Kampala, where he could swim in greater safety: no water snakes, parasites or unforeseen depths.

It was a notable day in his life when we moved into our garden house. There he found two graceful, maturely spreading mulberry bushes. These proved to have one obvious advantage and another quite unexpected. Their plentiful fruit was easily available to a small boy now just five who not only ate it but squashed it to produce "medicine" to treat his friends with. That was interesting enough; even more so was the fact that these bushes were home to chameleons. No doubt these patient, prehistoric-looking creatures were as surprised to discover Charles as he was to make the acquaintance of their rotating eyes, prehensile tail, and long, sticky tongue that uncurled and shot out to catch any fly nearby. Unprotestingly they transferred their grip from branch to his forefinger, presumably because he moved so much faster than they and increased their chance of dining in unusual places.

When he grew tired of transporting them and watching them turn colour as the background changed, he would park them back in their mulberry bush until another day. Meanwhile there were beautifully patterned butterflies to chase, always fruitlessly; gaudy, furry caterpillars to learn to keep away from, for touching them gave one an itchy rash; tadpoles to collect from the storm water drains. Up near the biology laboratories the boys discovered the scummy frog-pond. It was no trouble to squeeze through the fence, more difficult for them to avoid falling into the slimy green as they fished. Charles's reward, however, was to bring home a frog, put it in the bath, flush it down the drain, then rush outside to see it appear and catch it for a repeat performance. He had a small bike to ride with little fear of traffic. The old frangipani and paw-paw trees were easy to climb, yet far more interesting as he grew older was the roof.

With its fairly flat pitch, the runnels in the corrugated iron, so superior in this respect to Bangalore tiles, were ideal for trying out the speed of model cars or of mangoes, games that required a parental accomplice below since Nyesi refused to play them. Even parents were soon dispensed with. He found the flattest part of the roof, where he could test the speed of his black Jaguar with sprung wheels, his fastest model because its clearance was high enough to pass over the joins between the sheets of metal. Before any of this, however, he had to clear away accumulated bird droppings in the runnels. He remembers still, 40 years later, the smell of those droppings on the hot roof. Mangoes, we discovered, took a substantial and versatile place in a small boy's life. They could be rolled. They could be eaten, with the added satisfaction of making one stickily messy. If kept until rotten they could be thrown at a tree trunk to make a splashy explosion. When a friend, Tony Grigg, came over from Kenya to stay with us for a few days, we moved Charles out and gave our guest his room. Charles took the view that anyone who slept in his bed was a friend to be aided and protected, so he showed Tony his quick way of getting to the front of the house without using his bedroom's outer door or coming through our room: one simply climbed out of the window. Then with a rush of intimacy, Charles opened the bottom drawer of his chest. Tony was intrigued to find it full of mangoes. Charles explained: ammunition for pelting enemies. That, of course, meant friends.

Julia chose to be born on a night in 1956 when I was having to entertain Dr Radhakrishnan, then Vice-President of India, a dried-up man with nothing much to say. No doubt he was bored and would have preferred to do something other than eat dinner in the presence of two hundred red-gowned African students still governed colonially. Yet what such an old stick might have been doing is hard to imagine:

attending some equally boring function but in the liberated, marble grandeur of Delhi, possibly. Or mulling over the few less obscure points in the public lecture he had just delivered on "The Relation of the Soul with the Supreme"?

A decidedly concrete message was brought in to me that certain developments were imminent. I had to excuse myself, among many expressions of goodwill as the news spread down the long table. The Vice-President simply looked as sour as before and said nothing as I made my apologies. New life, he seemed to wish to convey down his nose, is of little consequence in the highest places. We made it up to Julia for this frigid international reception by flying out Charles's elegant, grey Silver Cross pram for her from England. With this to push, Nyesi attained unassailable prestige on the Hill. Her main attention was now transferred to the new baby: Charles, active, cheerful and friendly, began to learn that even freedom is qualified.

Julia's first contribution to life on the Hill was to invent an effective means of communication before she could talk. After experimenting for a time with baby crying and finding it at last banal, instead she would stand in her mahogany cot and run her plastic feeding bottle rhythmically back and forth across the vertical bars to protest against what she judged to be daily short rations. In no time, it seemed, this new toto was old enough to set off in fits and starts on her tricycle, attached by her cord to Nyesi's waist. More often than not she was barefoot, for in spite of all warnings she found her shoes too hot to keep on. As her freckled face showed, her hat too she used to push off. Past the spreading yellow and red hibiscus bushes, down the rutted murram path by the garden of succulents, she went out to play with the other two-year-olds. When we left East Africa she was coming up to three, solemnly interested in tadpoles, furry caterpillars, ants, chameleons and Charles's white mouse, which she delighted in seeing him put up my trouser leg. Although still too young to have attained her brother's status of free-ranging cyclist, she had exhibited a talent for abandoned dancing, once with the world (our globe) in her hand, to the accompaniment of Fats Waller's recording of "I'm gonna sit right down and write myself a letter". Such, alas, was the deplorable effect of the tropics on morals.

Chapter 4   Living Exotically

Dukas

Shopping in Kampala, preferably done in the early morning, afternoons in the town being too dazzlingly hot, was usually conducted
according to the eastern rite: one haggled over most things. In the
market, however, the heart of the town, one simply watched the quality
of what was offered. As elsewhere, the market served several purposes.
It was a place for eating: Africans with trays of sumbusas, curried and
hot, moved among the crowd. It was enjoyed for meeting friends and
for leisurely conversation, in Luganda especially so, because that
language's greetings and other formalities took so long and had to be
respected. Africans' sense of the use of time showed itself here as quite
different from Europeans', who tended to set about their shopping
briskly and were quick to leave. Then of course there were the African
stalls, with locally slaughtered meat, fish from the Lake, piles of green
oranges, grapefruit, limes, various bananas, breadfruit, cucumbers,
grenadillas, tomatoes, mangoes, paw-paw, Cape gooseberries, beans
both dried and green, plums and apples from Kenya, spices and nuts.
Around the few Asian stalls the ground was stained red with betel juice.
Stall-holders flicked away flies constantly with swats made of plaited
reeds or with a banana leaf.

Shopkeepers in the rest of town were mainly European or Asian,
more frequently the latter. A two-storey European department store,
Draper's, the largest shop in town, and a firm that sold British cars were
similar to those to be found in larger market towns in England. The

Asian shops (or "dukas"), however, were much more exotic and interesting. Take the Diamond Bakery – aptly named when you considered
the prices, said Makerere wives – for it was notorious for fleecing
bachelors. This duka sold general groceries. One went down two steps
to its dark-timbered building that looked so tumbledown because it was
never painted. Its sun-bleached, grey sign, hardly legible and tipsily
lopsided, was a carved piece of wood over the door, its faded paint
curled up in flakes. A leading competitor was run by two Asian brothers,
one of whom had a paunch so horizontally protuberant that he rested
his pad on it when writing the bill. To enter their duka, more recently
built, one went up two concrete steps with the eroded murram (red
gravel used for paths or road-surfaces) falling away on each side. This
was where my wife bought our groceries; Charles used to enjoy the
fresh, hot sumbusas (thin fried pastry envelopes with curried fillings)
that she brought home. An attractive cool duka, another step-down
one, was staffed by two very dark-skinned, soft-spoken Asian men. On
trestle tables they had hundreds of rolls of silk of all colours, from India
or China, the latter embroidered in the Chinese style familiar world-
wide. A very small shop, extremely popular with all races, was run by
a German couple who sold bedlinen, cheap towels, tablecloths and
sophisticated Swiss curtain materials. Small African shops would sell
cotton goods, particularly amerikani, plain white fabric useful for
uniforms, kanzus, curtains, bedcovers, in fact a tough, all-purpose,
mostly unbleached textile. Others had a good selection of cotton prints
for the dresses worn by prosperous African women such as Alisi and
Nyesi. Seven yards was the traditional amount needed for one such
dress: "Yardi saba, memsahib," Nyesi had called excitedly to remind us
once when we were going off to buy her a present.

A small group of women on the Hill, my wife among them, started
an association and published a newsletter that listed prices in the main
Asian shops. This was highly unpopular with the shopkeepers, the
Diamond Bakery in particular, but useful when my wife negotiated a
standing discount at her own grocer, one that she had to ask for nevertheless at each visit and repeatedly reaffirm. These dukas were often
ramshackle affairs, but all were crammed with goods, with barely a nod
in the direction of display. One simply went into the appropriate shop
through the scented haze from joss-sticks and asked for what one
wanted: drum of ghee, perhaps, excellent for roasting potatoes, or a
flask of Chianti, or jar of Bengal chutney, beach towels from Israel, or a

7lb tin of dried apricots from Australia. Most likely somewhere back in their organised disorder they would have it among the harvest of their international trade, waiting to be bargained for.

A different sort of shop was the one where the best barber in town, a pleasant sad-looking Asian, had his three chairs. Since he was a Moslem, Europeans tried to avoid going to him for a short back and sides during Ramadhan, because then his breath stank and he was deeply morose, suffering no doubt through the long hours of work until sunset and the next meal. Or possibly he was simply tired from staying up half the night eating. He would smile a little through his melancholy whenever I was sorry enough for him to let him practise his specialty, dry shampoo and scalp massage. His principal distinction, however, was that he displayed prominently for sale a mysterious liquid described by the labels on the bottles as "Hair and Brain Tonic".

For women there were two European hairdressers in Kampala. The one my wife went to had a combined dress and beauty shop. She was the only person we knew who had had anthrax: a scar from it marked her face. A good businesswoman, she kept her stock moving by regular sales and being open to bargaining: she also sold costume jewelry and gilded Indian leather sandals in various colours. Her sales technique could nevertheless be crude. Once she urged my wife to buy a girdle "to take off the inch" it would have needed to make a frock she was trying on fit. A girdle indeed! Such a constriction at the best of times, but in the heat of East Africa...!

Early one morning, with only Julia in the car (Charles had just been dropped off at school), my wife stopped for a minute to buy a loaf at the Atheneum, the Greek bakery. On the way in she passed a crippled, ragged African beggar sitting on the pavement, the only person in sight save for a small child with him. When she came out the child had gone, as had her handbag from the car. What made my wife suspect the beggar's complicity was the fact that he did not ask for money. When she reported the theft to the police, they thanked her for giving them their "first real lead": numerous thefts had taken place there. They then observed the cripple directing young children to steal from the cars parked unattended for the 60 seconds it took to run in and pick up a loaf.

We had to be alert too when, as happened occasionally, the shopping came to us. A persuasive Asian carpet trader, a grey-haired man of about fifty, would appear in the garden, his station-waggon loaded with rugs that he claimed had just come off a dhow at Mombasa.

Perhaps some had. When he knew us better he revealed that he repre-
sented a carpet factory in Pakistan. In no time he would scatter piles of
his wares temptingly on the grass, nothing too much trouble. Whether
we bought one or not, he would drive away equally satisfied at having
displayed his virtuosity. In fact, we were lucky to get from him a "Rose
Khirman", two "Princess Bokharas" and a couple of others, for after we
left we heard that prices had shot up. He was never keen, he told us as
we got to know him, to try to sell to Bernard de Bunsen. We already
understood why. Bernard had in his house valuable rugs that his mother
had bought many years before in Persia. These set a standard that the
trader knew he could not compete with. One evening this poor man,
normally cheerful and imperturbably obliging, arrived in our garden
greatly and indignantly distressed. He had just come from another
house on the Hill where, in return for showing his carpets, he had been
shocked to receive homosexual advances. We could easily imagine the
carpets laid out for display, since we knew the house, but could form
for ourselves no picture at all of whatever our colleague had got up to.
"Must have been drinking", we thought. In our innocence the best we
could do for our genuinely distressed Asian friend was offer him the
Anglo-Indian remedy for countless ills, a cup of tea. This he sorrowfully
refused.

In Kampala there was a shop called Shankardass where we went to
buy LP vinyl gramophone records. To our horror we found when we
got them home that despite their plastic inner jackets they were gritty,
either from the dust in the town or because they had been played often
before with steel needles, or both. We tried washing them in the bath:
no change. We hung one of our woollen runners, tightly woven by
Arizona Indians, over our loudspeaker cabinet, as we already did for our
old Caruso and Nellie Melba seventy-eights. That cut out the crackle
but also muffled the sound. In the end, desperate as we were for music,
we learned to put up with the sort of noise that on the wireless used to
be called atmospherics. We came to associate the grit with the performance on certain records. Shankardass, for some reason, kept a
gratifying amount of Gabriel Fauré. Had some lonely District Officer in
the dry heat of the sandy north, also devoted to Fauré's evocative
music, sold his used records to Shankardass? Perhaps the naked
Karamojong, thinking such elegant sounds a sort of magic, had for their
own inscrutable purposes stood about listening too? These LPs, sec-
ondhand or not, we could not resist. Long ago we threw them away,

38

when they were worn truly beyond patience, beyond remedy of the lightest and most up-to-date stylus. Yet even now I can hear Gérard Souzay's wonderful phrasing of "Hélas, j'ai dans le coeur une tristesse affreuse" but sounding as though he were standing outside, recording for Decca in a sandstorm.

Gradually our meals took on the style and flavours of East Africa, as well as certain fortuitous international features. For breakfast, most Europeans found that the longer they stayed the less could they stomach bacon and eggs or other foundations of Edwardian *embonpoint*. Sausages, in particular, we soon gave up. They came out of a tin and lay on the plate looking flayed: instead, slices of paw-paw (papaya), said to be an excellent aid to digestion, small bananas the size of a finger, and freshly-squeezed orange juice from ripe, green fruit that had not been dyed. Toast, marmalade, and coffee might be preceded, if one could tolerate such an enormity, by a boiled egg. Lunch, too, was light. An avocado pear, a salad (some people insisted on having theirs washed in a solution of potassium permanganate; we used the municipal tap water, at that time safe), some cheese and rolls, then mangoes and passion fruit or the dried apricots from Australia soaked and cooked, or mulberries from the garden. We drank no alcohol at lunch.

After that, no siesta either, in spite of the advice we had been given in London, but back to the office, where the temperature would by now be well up in the eighties. Afternoon tea was very simple; frequently we had visitors, often Africans. Then later – when the children had had their supper and enjoyed their splash-about bath with one of us, when we had read or told them their bedtime stories – after all this happy time, now that it was past seven, quite dark, with cicadas screeching, we changed and began our own evening together. Alisi would come in and with her smallest voice tell my wife that dinner was ready: "Chagula tayari, memsahib".

With dinner the most substantial meal of the day we had things the wrong way round, said the physicians. We should eat our heaviest meal at noon, then a very light supper later. Good advice but useless, for had we followed it the afternoons would have been scandalously somnolent in our 7.30am to 4.00pm workday. Before dinner we would normally have drunk Schweppes tonic water, with limes but no gin, and eaten peanuts and banana crisps. For anyone who happened to drop in, there would have been beer from the Nile Brewery. Dinner would begin with soup or fruit, go on to fillet of beef, say, with sweet potatoes roasted in ghee, stuffed tomatoes and green beans from Kenya. After that, pineapple, possibly, or the fruit salad made by all African cooks on the Hill as a matter of course: oranges, Cape goose-berries, passion fruit, bananas, pineapple, mulberries, grapefruit.

When we wanted wine we usually drank Chianti (Ruffino) because it travelled well and was easy to get in the dukas. Choice of meat was poor: locally slaughtered beef, frequently available, was still warm when bought in the market or, as little Martin Tenniswood's mother Audrey put it, "still quivering". We became so tired of beef (a complete fillet cost 7 shillings 50 cents) that we did not buy it for some years after we left East Africa. Scrawny chickens, too, could usually be found. Sometimes there would be pork or lamb from Kenya.

"Facing Mount Kenya"

My wife took a break from her career while we were in East Africa, in order to have our family and be with the children while they were very young. Nevertheless she stepped in from time to time, as did many on the Hill, to help with whatever needed to be done. One of her adven-tures was a brief stint as part-time manager of the college bookshop, under the general guidance of the Rev. Fred Welbourn (of whom more later); he was already involved in it in addition to his normal duties. Neither had had experience of business, but they managed to do the job. However, there were unexpected distractions. Here, then, is another of my wife's after-dinner tales.

"We should not have been as surprised as we were because, after all, the bookshop is well down the Hill, easily accessible not only to students but, intentionally, to people from Kampala as well. Off the main road and secluded, attractively we have always thought, it stands down there quietly among the trees: too quietly, evidently. It wasn't long before I wished it had been put somewhere more open. On one occasion, two Africans from town, wearing suits and those little round skull caps that seem to be *de rigueur* for aspiring politicians, came in and stood about as though waiting for someone. After a while I realised that they thought I was a customer. They were waiting for me to leave! In fact I heard them ask the African assistant who I was. His reply obviously discouraged them, as did my evident suspicions, because they left without saying any more or buying anything.

"Then there was the unconnected but still disturbing case of the bicycle. It was bookshop property. Fred had bought it for the assistant, to get him around the Hill quickly when he went to collect orders or make deliveries. Well, the other day it was stolen, and Fred had a shrewd idea who had taken it. But he didn't want to call in the police – you know how kind-hearted he is – preferring to allow the man a few days before trying to make him give it back.

"These were both pointers to the way things might go, so we shouldn't have been surprised yesterday morning. All the same, it was a shock to arrive and find the door broken open. Inside, what a mess! Books pulled off the shelves and scattered; on the floor a sticky puddle and large prints of bare feet leading from it. You see, the bookshop for some reason sells Coca-Cola too. The burglars had taken most of the cases but some bottles they had drunk on the spot: broken off the necks and splashed them about. This time Fred agreed that we should call the police.

"Eventually an African constable arrived, a Protectorate Policeman who spoke some English. He brought with him a standard enquiry sheet. Apparently this required him, first, to take my fingerprints. When he had done so he proceeded to the questions, all addressed to me rather than to the matter of the burglars.

"'Who is your chief?'

"This I found difficult. I did not want to strain credibility by pointing out that I had no chief. Then should I say Bernard de Bunsen, or the Governor, possibly? To put the matter beyond dispute I answered, 'Queen Elizabeth the Second'.

"This must have satisfied him because he wrote it down carefully and went on, 'Where is your ggombolola?' (A Buganda local government unit.)

"Fortunately I knew what this meant, although it applied no more than the first question.

"'Makerere,' I answered. This too he accepted.

"'Have you any marks on your body?' he then asked, apparently in all seriousness, and with a suggestive flourish of his hands.

"'No!!!'

"'Now I have to write down here your description,' he continued, and looked me up and down appraisingly.

"I awaited his verdict with some concern.

"'Strong building,' he concluded.

"Pleased with the sound of it he said, 'I will write down strong building'.

"He did so, definitively.

"My criminal record now presumably complete, he made no investigation of the scene of the crime but instructed me to let him know later what was missing from the shop. Then he left us to the task of cleaning up and finding out. The odd thing is this: the only books missing, when we had taken stock, were Jomo Kenyatta's *Facing Mount Kenya*, all our copies.

"Shortly after these adventures in crime the bookshop moved to safer quarters in the Administration Building."

Pastimes

To go away on safari was refreshing, yet on our return to Makerere we always enjoyed the happy feeling of coming home to a distinct and congenial community. Much serious work was accomplished there; one could also relax with friends and colleagues. Often we gave dinner parties or went out to dine at other houses on the Hill or in Kampala (only rarely to Uganda Government people at Entebbe), for this was the commonest form of social amusement among expatriates. True, there was a cinema in town that alternated its programme between European films and lurid Asian epics (Africans for this purpose were Europeans) but frequently the film was uninteresting. In any case it started late, so that anyone who went to it looked pale with fatigue next day. At least they had not had to dress incongruously, as report had it that Europeans did down in Salisbury, Southern Rhodesia, where the women were said to show off in evening gowns from Paris as they sat in the front rows of wooden seats. There were clubs in Kampala, of which more shortly, but Makerere people made little use of them. A group on the Hill offered the opportunity of amateur theatricals to those who had the talent and even, to judge by results, to the desperate who had none. Too infrequently Miss Yvonne Catterall (Mrs Hugh Dinwiddy) would give a much-appreciated piano recital. A circle dozed through members' papers and discussed them desultorily. Visiting lecturers held forth occasionally. One professor thought to give his inaugural lecture the day before he retired.

Threatened with this plethora of exciting diversions, a few on the Hill allowed themselves to venture into affairs. No matter how discreetly they conducted themselves they had no hope of remaining unobserved. Scrutiny was intense, comment detailed. Yet so transported were those involved, so inappropriately secure did they feel as they openly communicated private significance with their eyes or an inclination of the head, that they would saunter in the merciless sunlight like actors on a stage, going nowhere in particular but in a definite direction. Not they but their neglected spouses looked ill at ease. Gossip, feeding fantasy, invested past Makerere lovers with extraordinary qualities, with epic powers or weaknesses. She, we were told again and again of someone no longer on the Hill (we caught a glimpse of her once when she came back, looking sad and faded), was a sorceress who used to float diaphanously about, supercharged, needing only to smile and beckon. He (we saw him only once, too, showing fatigue), a victim, folly readily bewitched, was nonetheless dashing, the eternally handsome youth.

Not such promising material for the ancient game of myth-making, the couples under current observation, fitted out from a wardrobe of stock, were reported to have based their affairs on mysterious, permissive pacts with their spouses, not known in detail but analysed at length. Or shadowy pasts gilded their involvement, with hints of liaisons with foreign royalty on discreet, between-the-wars Mediterranean islands. In fact, these blithe subjects of myth and fantasy differed not greatly, if at all, from their observers, save in their having chosen by chance the most banal of distractions. There were many on the Hill, of course, who neither gossiped much nor erred, but soberly sought confinement in their work. Our neighbour, Kenneth Baker, for example, after solitary dinner each evening, went to bed immediately to sleep for an hour or two, then got up and laboured on virtuously into the small hours.

Most, faithful spouses, devoted themselves to each other, difficult though that was to imagine, sometimes, when one saw them together. One couple made a point of letting everyone know how fervently, how anxiously they were hoping to conceive. The Hill waited. A sardonic colleague, who knew his London fish and chips, said they might as well have put out a sign at their bungalow: "Trying tonight". Over all this marital harmony and discord the remote unworldly bachelor, Bernard de Bunsen, presided like a benevolent Puritan. He seemed to see nothing yet grasped surprisingly acutely whatever was going on. Of one woman, who appeared wearing exotically long earrings and with her hair swinging loosely when her errant husband came back to her, he said disapprovingly that she was "flaunting her reunion".

Dinner parties could be interesting in various ways. One met people from the Hill and in government service, people in business or church, official and private visitors from Britain (many) or the other East African territories (fewer) or the United States (very few), as well as missionaries, teachers or doctors in from their stations. Even those from the Hill were a great variety, given the college's spread of faculties. Richard Hartland-Rowe, in zoology, would be just back from a research expedition to some far-off lake that no-one else had even heard of. Hugh Trowell, physician, would speak from long experience of the African children's disease of kwashiorkor (in 1935 misdiagnosed at Mulago Hospital as hereditary syphilis): once weaned, and fed on a diet deficient in both calories and protein, as was commonly the case in the steamier tropics, babies would be marked with brown hair and bulging bellies. If they survived they would lack for life the resistance and energy of others better fed in childhood. Then he would elaborate the theory that we Europeans, by contrast, were all condemned to fat because we consumed cow's milk and, worse, fed it to our infants.

Aidan Southall and Peter Gutkind knew in arresting detail about the mixed African urban population around Kampala. Victor Temple, bubbling with goodwill, nevertheless could not get his tongue around a certain student's name, Kyewalabye, and settled cheerfully for "Ky-wallabee", which the student was in fact delighted with. Charles Tenniswood, in chemistry, could explain exactly why a new medical laboratory at Mulago had blown up. Freddie Sutton, the Assistant Bursar, was enlightening on how the Tanganyika groundnuts scheme had collapsed: one of the survivors, he was a good-natured, short, springy and energetic man. Once, just back from leave in England, he told us how hard-up his friends and peers there were: they "couldn't afford to have a drink every evening, a pint of beer or glass of sherry".

The Bursar, John Burroughs, when in the King's African Rifles, had helped subdue the Italian armies in Somaliland and Ethiopia. Fergus Wilson, Dean of Agriculture and Forestry, was expert on trees. At the slightest hint of a request he would next evening kindly turn up with assistants to plant a lovely something or other that would grow astonishingly fast. There was the physician who put a coffee spoonful of brandy in his baby's feeding bottle for the long flight to England; another suffered the appalling distinction of having his wife die suddenly in bed beside him one night. Anthony Low and Kenneth Ingham, historians, felicitously related no matter what to East Africa's past, while their colleague Ray Beachey, a gentle Canadian, encouraged us to go to his homeland even though when he returned there himself he found he could no longer stand the place, in particular the sight of earmuffs at the onset of winter. Lalage Bown and Ieuan Hughes, extra-mural tutors, would come down from the north-east or over from Kenya with their unique knowledge of the people they worked among. Here now was Marjorie Baker back from a journey across the Pacific on a slow, Japanese liner on which nobody else understood English and she no Japanese.

Mix this random sprinkling from Makerere with the occasional senior or junior government officer from any of the three territories; or settler politicians; or with William Clarke of *The Observer* and Members of Parliament from Westminster; or academic personages such as tough, shrewd, lovable old Lillian Penson, former Vice-Chancellor of the University of London, endearingly and with good reason known as Cocktail Lil; or David Lindsay Keir, Master of Balliol, whom we caught peeping into his constitutional history on our shelves to look for signs of our having read it; or with the Anglican Bishop Brown of Uganda or the new Roman Catholic chaplain, the Reverend Father P.D. Foster OP, urbane but severely aware that he had come out to replace a predecessor whispered to have transgressed in some Catholic fashion; or Thomas Hodgkin, charming, brilliant but naively and conspiratorially leftist, now recently arrived on a visit from West Africa, somewhat startled to find himself sitting next to Sue Still of the American Red Cross, a stout woman who could be relied upon to proclaim with a formidable chuckle that bed was her favourite piece of furniture, meaning only that she liked to sleep; or there were the Bauers, a Swiss couple down on their luck, whom a charitable East African Airways pilot had smuggled out of Ethiopia, where the Emperor's treasury had been too empty to pay them their contractual salary and his officials too negligent to find their confiscated passports; or Peter Kibblewhite, of Callender's Cables, responsible for building power lines across Uganda from the Jinja dam, and even John Stonehouse (later MP), then starting his climb to notoriety by organising co-operatives in Uganda and getting into trouble with the protectorate authorities for allowing his directors to live with their hands in the till. Soon he was required to leave Uganda under escort, for his own protection said the government, its diplomacy unconsciously prophetic. With such a mixture for company, all would agree, our social life was hardly dull. Lucy Sutherland had said arrogantly at Oxford, when advising me not to take up my appointment in the British Foreign Service, "you'll find the company better in academic life," yet I doubt if she had had anywhere quite like Makerere in mind.

Some other features of dinner parties we found pleasant. Conversation there was, predominantly political rather than aesthetic or intellectual, and of course gossip in abundance, but the food, too, was often worth noticing. Coming to East Africa seemed to have shaken the British out of the wartime cottage pie into which their cooking had sagged, if it had ever been anything but despondent. The presence of wives from other parts of Europe helped. Clorinda Gale, from Naples, earned everyone's gratitude by initiating us all into the true, deep-crust pizza. Marie Boshoff, who kept her sharp Swiss tongue in practice by uninhibitedly attacking men's sexual vanities, applied its bright blade to those whose culinary standards lagged, and showed them how to improve. A Swedish couple in the International Confederation of Free Trade Unions introduced their superb Sophiacake. One of our African cooks, in the days before Alisi, had learnt from someone how to make a good Espagnole sauce, half way to a demi-glace. Americans, too, brought with them their own specialties. When it came to the Fourth of July, however, the genial US consul, Charles Hooper, was never allowed to provide alcohol at his reception. Fear of multi-racial drinking? By his Government's arcane methods of financing he had barely enough money for food and soft drinks: they ran out once.

Perhaps the most interesting thing about Makerere cuisine was the tradition of curries. No one person was responsible for that. It resulted, no doubt, from various influences: there was the long connexion with India; the good ingredients available in the Asian dukas; African cooks learned it from various sources and passed it on; people expected it, in the absence of any particularly interesting African cuisine, as appropriately exotic. Nobody would have thought of serving it without the full range of side dishes: peanuts and other nuts, diced pineapple, several chutneys, grated coconut, sliced mangoes and paw-paw, tomato salad, sliced cucumber, banana rounds, sultanas, diced apple.

Of all the meals we enjoyed, curry seemed most in tune with the houseboys' customary dress when serving at table. The long, clean, white kanzu, below which could be seen spreading bare feet, would be held in by a broad cummerbund, usually red but occasionally green, very rarely some other colour (in an hotel we once saw black and in another, looking precious, royal blue). On the head, a fez of matching colour. The fez may sound a simple sort of hat to wear but this is not so. A slight tilt forward and it looks ridiculous: if backward, it becomes derisory; a minute tilt to one side may be thought becoming but go half an inch too far and the wearer looks inexperienced; another half inch, tipsy. Protectorate Policemen's authority required their black fez to be perfectly vertical. Had he not been subjected to Alisi's and Nyesi's mocking laughter, Abunwazi would have worn his red one both tilted back and over too far to the side, which made him look astonished. Some fezzes, we were embarrassed to observe since we thought it excessive in civilian life, were adorned with the bwana's regimental badge (in such cases, no doubt, bwana mkubwa was expected, not merely "lord" but "great lord"); this was becoming less frequent in the fifties.

That houseboys should wear white gloves when serving was also dying out. Hostesses simply got them to wash their hands. Feet remained silently bare, widely spread from not wearing shoes: advantages, no bunions and no squeaks. African servants enjoyed the formality and the occasion. On the whole they were skilful and remarkably dignified. From time to time we gave or were invited to a dinner in honour of a distinguished visitor. Here is what we served for one such, when Christopher Cox, from the Colonial Office, dined with us in December 1957: cream of tomato soup, with a dry sherry; paupiettes de veau clementine, creamed spinach, carrots, whipped mashed potatoes, turnips, green beans, with Chianti; banana creole (with rum, molasses and nuts) and ice cream; cheese and pressed dates; fruit (Kenya plums, tangerines, pineapple, passion fruit); coffee and liqueurs. With due respect for hierarchy, Cox wrote to say that it was the best meal not served in a Government House that he had ever had in East Africa! In Kenya, first and second toasties (canapes) would have been served with drinks before dinner. The usual habit in Uganda was to serve peanuts which the cook had just tossed in ghee in the frying pan, a dish, warm, for each guest; on special occasions we would serve one set of toasties as well before dinner.

Dinner parties might be like that or run of the mill, but each one was interrupted by a strange ritual, a rational and useful procedure, but still strange. After dinner and before coffee the hostess would invite the women to withdraw to the bedrooms to use whatever facility the house had, usually not more than one. At the same time the host would suggest that the men "see Africa". This incantation was invariable. In response the men would troop out into the dark garden, stand in a sometimes longish row among the random gleams of fire-flies, and pee together on the grass beneath the brilliant and unfamiliarly distributed stars. Some, particularly the hearty sort, took schoolboyish delight in this, others less, but all went out. Bernard de Bunsen would always stand back a little from the rest and wait, not peeing but looking as though he were distantly contemplating the immensity of the universe. At a settlers' dinner in Kenya, while the men were thus occupied the women would be shuttling to and fro with a hurricane lantern to sit in turns over a deep pit.

All these dinners were given by Europeans virtually exclusively for Europeans. We did invite the few African members of faculty and some Africans from the town or the countryside nearby, but they seemed not to relax or enjoy themselves; they rarely returned an invitation. In fact, as far as the Baganda were concerned, all outsiders found them difficult to meet socially: few succeeded in getting to know any of them intimately. On the other hand, Africans, whether students or others, seemed greatly to enjoy coming to tea, and always preferred being out in the garden to indoors. They liked the informality, with Charles clowning about and a simple (but abundant – Alisi saw to that) provision of tea, cake and sandwiches. In the scented shade they relaxed with us and chatted, as we could then do all the more comfortably ourselves. With one or two exceptions, our African guests retained, nevertheless, a level of reserve. It was our life, ourselves, that they wanted to know about. That we were equally interested in them and theirs they found difficult to believe. In fact, questions made them suspicious. One shy teacher and extra-mural student from the west, Yunia Ganyana, whom we got to know in this way, did however write to say that she had learnt from us that an African could feel at home with an English person. As always, in small things much is revealed.

"How to treat Africans?" seemed to us an unfortunate question, although we heard it often. It both presupposed and encouraged mistakes: for example, the opinion that beyond recognition of their custom Africans needed some special condescension rather than common civility. From naive visitors one heard praise for East African "friendliness". This supposed merit they seemed to find among Europeans and Africans, but not Asians. In any case it was an illusion generated by nameless fears. What could they have expected? Civility would be a better description of what visitors found, and is a sounder basis for complex society than is casual friendliness. Each African tribe had its courtesies, some more elaborate than others, as was also the case with the various groups among the Europeans. Inter-racial civility had to grow from these. That informed observer Noni Crosfield (see Chapter 7) thought Kampala's success in this respect unimpressive compared with her own experience of South Africa. Yet what had been achieved by the rapidly changing times of the fifties, if no longer the so-called "Happy Uganda" of the early colonisers, was tolerable and workable while the British peace endured.

There were no Asians among the teaching staff or administrators at Makerere. Whether Hindus, Sikhs, Moslems or Christians, Asians enjoyed their own society, their clubs, schools and festivals, distinct from those of Europeans or Africans. For Diwali the Hindus strung lights everywhere; for another of their holy festivals they cheerfully splashed each other with coloured water. In spite of their separateness, the races generally got on tolerably well day-to-day. That is, if one did not expect some unreasonably blissful harmony, some millennial removal of human friction. Although the races might treat each other with less than polished courtesy in shops or offices, it remained true that commercial and official Kampala had no colour bar. Any shop at any time might contain customers of any race. Clubs, as we shall see, were a different matter.

Africans, largely ignorant of commerce, undoubtedly believed that Asian traders were exploiting them, but so far resentment had risen only infrequently to a dangerous level. What is more, Africans equally regarded African traders as dishonest, just as both Baganda and immigrant tribes (among all of whom there was no "African" solidarity) openly recognised the gross corruption and incompetence of the Buganda Government. Some Protectorate Government officers believed that racial tensions between Africans and Asians were a serious danger as self-government approached: they hoped that continuing expansion of Islam, embracing both races, might ease them. Others thought this a vain hope because Moslems were no more united than any other religious group. What was more, Africans generally mistrusted and feared them, for Moslems were widely regarded as sorcerers. In Tanganyika the official doctrine seemed to be that because racial harmony was desirable, it must exist. Yet when I was in Dar-es-Salaam, Nicholas Muriuki (a former Makerere student from Kenya, then starting his career with the Shell Company), warned me that Africans there were far more racially discontented than official statements on multi-racialism recognised. It is generally true, no doubt, that the privileged underestimate the depth of resentment among the less fortunate.

On all sides, moreover, one encountered embarrassing remnants of long-standing, foolishly petty attitudes of colour-sensitivity and exclusion. For example, in November 1956 I met a European official in Dar-es-Salaam who, when in a former post out in a district, had reputedly "gone native". That phrase was actually used by my informant, a very senior European in the Tanganyika public service, who thought himself obliged to explain that this man had married an African woman, had had several "black children", and lived a social life entirely separated from his colleagues. Perhaps that was what he wanted? But if so, precisely why?

There was also reported to me, on another occasion, the case of a European official who was going to "have to go" because she was "sleeping with Africans". Possibly my informant would have found more palatable the knowledge being gained *en passant* by our Makerere researchers that some African women openly acknowledged their desire for European men. Like so many racial questions, these sexual ones carried a heavy load of ambiguity. Conventional nineteenth-century British middle-class morality was surviving uncomfortably into changing times.

Given the stark layers of economic and cultural difference between the races, however, and the divisions within each of the legal groupings of "Asian" and "African" (for clearly, to state a legal category is not necessarily to create a community), it should seem surprising that under the colonial peace the races worked together in joint interests as often as they did. In Tanganyika, for example, a couple of years before independence, elected members of various races, all there because supported by the Tanganyika African National Union, were co-operating effectively as an Opposition in the Legislative Council. Certainly race relations differed from territory to territory, and even from region to region. Cultural misunderstandings and prejudices flourished inventively. Yet people of different race frequently got on as well as, perhaps better than, it was reasonable to expect, however much they felt at ease or resentful in ignoring each other socially. In Uganda, nevertheless, this failure, as some saw it, to achieve a multi-racial intimacy of the sort that each race was alleged to enjoy within itself, many Europeans both at Makerere and in government found disturbing.

Clubs and Snobs

The Kampala Club admitted only Europeans. Consequently (but unreasonably, some of its members argued) it was held up by those who advocated social multi-racialism as a standing proof of its members' lack of goodwill towards other races. Asian clubs, no less exclusive, were not subject to similar criticism. This was probably because Europeans tended to regard Ugandan Asians ("not the best sort of Indian", as one commonly heard it said) as not counting in the same way as themselves or Africans. They saw Asians, unthinkingly, as not worth knowing and hardly worth envying, as the sort of people whom one expected to stay apart, to feel and to have no responsibility for civilising themselves. Be that as it may, the Kampala Club had come to seem to many, Europeans and Africans, to stand for shameful attitudes. It did not represent all Europeans. Few Makerere people belonged to it, not because we all stayed out on principle, although many did, but because we made a sort of club among ourselves away on our Hill: in any case most could not afford the high fees.

To remedy this imagined plight of poorer Europeans, the even poorer educated Africans, and the Asians, who were assumed to feel spurned whether they were rich, some very, or poor, the Uganda Government set up and subsidised a new club. It offered accommodation and full dining facilities, with membership open to all races at low fees. Thus it was to be something more than the United Kenya Club in Nairobi, a successful multi-racial venture limited to Wednesday luncheon meetings. Together with some other Europeans from Makerere (there was no overwhelming rush) we joined this Uganda

Club dutifully, even idealistically. Some African professionals, dignitaries and faculty members joined too. Asians, exclusively the rich or politically prominent, also came forward, not to be outdone in this overt act of goodwill. Senior British officials signed on as a matter of policy. Visitors from Britain, passing through, sagaciously pronounced themselves impressed with this imaginatively enlightened departure, as in their uninformed enthusiasm they saw it. They placed great hope in the grand premises impeccably decorated in colours so inoffensive, armchairs and sofas off-white, that nobody was expected to feel affronted. Service and food, also bland but acceptable in a good cause, were adequate. In deference to groups that for religious reasons did not drink alcohol, or were supposed not to, there was no bar. The possibility did not escape critics that anxious officialdom had been glad to veto alcohol for fear of unwelcome verities that might be all too forthcoming if inhibitions weakened. No matter: on spotlessly white tablecloths new silverware gleamed an invitation to the members' jolly multi-racial presence.

There was one snag. Like the railway station at Adlestrop, it was only a name, nobody came. Persistent attempts to dine there found us in marble halls that were hollower than empty, with perhaps at most three other members or guests. No matter how close the evening, the club sat deserted under a dismal, lonely chill. Cheerful resolution petered out as one suffered through the death of yet another illusion. After a while we gave up; so did most others. As practice had already proved, the races could get on approximately well during the day doing whatever had to be done. In the evening they were happy, indeed determined, to separate. For if any human activity is to be called natural, surely a strong candidate must be the virtually universal preference for the ease, the casual subtleties, the wit, of one's own language.

Our subsequent experience of another effort at mixing was just as disappointing. We eventually decided that it was ridiculous to go all the way to Kenya to see a dentist. Since there were qualified Asian dentists in Kampala, why not try one of them? We did, and found him congenial. As patients of an Asian dentist we were, I believe, unique among Europeans. Only later, in North America, was it revealed to us how backward professionally he must have been, but in Kampala we were happily ignorant of that. To be fair, he did say frankly that he was unable to repair my wife's tooth that had been broken when we skidded off the muddy road near Lake Bunyonyi. On learning that we enjoyed curries he invited us to dinner to try some other Indian food. We gladly accepted and found that we were to be alone with him and his wife. The food was delicious. We liked each other. Everything looked auspiciously set for friendship. Yet when we got back to Makerere we felt exhausted. There had been no carefree talk. Things had been said as though prescribed by a formula, straying from which would have resulted in disaster. We had watched them watching us as one would, carefully, if a guest turned out not to be *homo sapiens*. Symbolic of the mortifying force of our emotions, which took us by surprise, was our memory of having been disconcerted, when we arrived, to see the dinner plates set out inverted on the table. We turned them over at a signal from our host. Throughout the meal he waved flies away from the food. What possible reasonable argument could be assembled against inverting dinner plates if one wanted to, we asked ourselves later. Yet how foreign those plates had seemed, because so many other differences, invisible and greater, spread out from them and, despite goodwill, subverted relaxation. How humiliating to have to confront one's own rigidities!

Was it simply the case that Europeans, particularly the British, were too weighed down with social snobbery, brought out from home with colour-prejudice and all their other complex baggage from the history of empire? This we asked ourselves without conviction, aware that it was the stock question but by now familiar enough with East Africa to doubt the expected response. Americans, Swedes, Swiss encountered obstacles to their goodwill analogous to our own. The Portuguese, we sometimes heard, made a better job of race relations. This assertion ignored the brutal Portuguese record on the East African coast during their ascendancy there, and seemed in the modern imagination to be exclusively a matter of who had been sleeping with whom. Certainly the Goans in Kampala, a distinct, well-educated community, had charming manners, delicate hands and Portuguese names. These merits were presumably the product of several centuries, however, not an example of instant rapport. The Baganda, we noticed, cherished their own snobberies and in this art needed no instruction from the British. They marked off among themselves lines hardly visible to other races, or other tribes, but of desperate social significance to them. To their own people they habitually adopted class-conscious speech. To superiors a convoluted, servile style, to inferiors a no-nonsense curtness that suggested what it must have been like when Normans hectored Anglo-Saxons.

Some upper-class Baganda owned property in the slum villages around Kampala and resisted taxation for municipal improvement while living themselves on their country estates. Yet from their assumed vantage of moral superiority they deplored the low behaviour and social status of the slum-dwellers which by their exploitation they had helped to create. The Baganda in general, themselves far from paragons, looked down snobbishly on other tribes as uncivilised, as barbarians who got into fights and took to thieving and prostitution when they moved into town. A Muganda would have no scruples about haughtily addressing a member of a supposedly less sophisticated tribe as "Savage!". One Muganda made that distinction in a conversation with Elspeth Huxley. Unselfconsciously he told her that people from Ruanda were not civilised like Baganda but were only savages. On Kilimanjaro I heard that the Chagga people used the same style in their occasional relations with the wilder tribes on the plains below.

What of small incidents such as the following? When my wife's string of beads broke and scattered one day, a Muganda ex-chief standing nearby called to her reprovingly that she must not stoop or kneel to pick them up. That was a task for a servant but would be degrading for her, he said. This man was "Custodian" of a Hall of Residence: he could not be called "Porter", as some from Oxford wished, because "porter" in East Africa had come to mean "unskilled labourer". Was this admirable, dignified ex-chief a snob? As for greater inhumanities, simplifiers forgot how appalled the early European explorers in East Africa were to discover that even some of the African slaves owned slaves. Asians in general, throughout East Africa, showed no sign (save for their sporadic taking of mistresses or consorting with prostitutes) of yearning for the society of Africans, whom they dismissed as primitive, or for that of Europeans, whom they tolerated as a useful evil. Arabs down on the coast and in Zanzibar kept to their own ways. The Masai, still nobly apart in their courageous, traditional life and aware of their warrior history, remained contemptuous of everyone else. This despite the fact that their young men and women were increasingly infected with East Africa's common scourge, venereal disease. Some of the Americans and South Africans whom we met were racially snobbish, others not. Of course, intolerable snobs of all stripes could be found among the British, to whom generally the affliction seemed to come as naturally, severe or slight, as the common cold. Yet more were substantially free of the taint because interested heart and soul in the job they had come out to do. Alas for any simple answer or expedient, it was all much too complicated to be explained, even more to be altered, by anyone in a hurry. As that wise liar Rousseau knew, in the beginning was the word, and the word was snob, the corroding, detrimental comparison that came in with the first stirrings of social display and difference. With such a snobbish gene making its fertile mischief universally, efforts to remedy some particular shape of its achievement tend to be lost in the general waste. Too fast, then, and one could only distort on this field of social battle where reason was always unwelcome while feelings, whether of hurt and envy or of fear and advantage, stubbornly upheld their selfish claims.

Since snobbery remains systematically impossible to define, save in the most general terms, what one might say is that amidst such a confusion of standards of every kind it was all the more important to be strictly honest with oneself about one's feelings. Not that feelings alone justify conduct, yet they can hardly be sublimated successfully within principle if they remain obscure. Truth to tell, because of her delicate temperament and because my wife enjoyed serious conversation daily with her, we felt more sympathetically intimate with Alisi than with many whom we found ourselves sitting next to at those amusing, all-European dinner parties, or with any Asian. On the other hand, we could not have kept up our European pace of work without the support of friendships that we made among our Makerere colleagues. Also important to us was the encouragement offered by visitors from Britain such as Richard Livingstone, Christopher Cox or Eric Ashby, whose conversation brought it home that, because of the many channels of imperial connexion, we were not holed up, abandoned, in some irremediably perplexing tropical backwater, some "outpost of progress".

An East African Mrs Beeton's

We found it a test of our own understanding to read *The Kenya Settlers' Cookery Book and Household Guide*. First published in 1928, it was frank about its objective: to give "assistance to newcomers to the Colony, to young or inexperienced housekeepers, and to bachelor settlers in Kenya, who must often find themselves obliged to put up with incompetency on the part of untrained native cooks or houseboys". In 1936 a companion handbook, in Swahili, had come out for those African cooks, containing recipes and "good advice" on personal and kitchen cleanliness. By the time we bought the book in 1953 it was proudly in its eleventh edition (1951). It claimed, truly, to be known everywhere in Kenya and to have a regular sale in Uganda.

Why had it proved so popular? Its nearly 300 pages of recipes covered a great range and took account of local conditions, so were invaluable. In our edition an article had been added on the use and care of electric cookers and washing machines, since wood stoves were starting to be replaced. The "Hints for Safari", a formidably practical and detailed warning to the feckless or inexperienced, listed 58 items to take, not including the medicine chest.

The housewife who finds herself responsible for getting a safari ready will find it best to prepare a careful list of everything necessary beforehand, and to check off the list as the packing proceeds. This list should be kept for future occasions, and augmented or altered as experience suggests. A boy who has been on safari is a great help, as he generally knows what is required, but even the best boy should be supervised. Careful, well thought out packing makes a difference to the number of boxes required, and to the speed with which camp can be struck. It really pays to have a special place in each chop box for each thing, and to insist that the boys return things to their proper places. This saves confusion in the small space at one's disposal in a tent, and also saves time and worry in searching for things.

The cook can usually be trusted to look after his kitchen necessities, but it is wise to see for oneself that nothing has been omitted. He will require clean petrol tins for heating water, and if there is no safari oven another tin for use as such; a bucket, a frying pan, a set of five or six sufurias [metal cooking pots], fitting into one another, lids for these, or sufficient tin plates to serve the purpose, bread, or cake tins, a washing up bowl, a mixing bowl, a strainer, kitchen knife, fork, spoons, a charcoal iron, matches, soap, dish cloths, etc (see list).

As eggs are often broken on a rough trip, some should be boiled at home, then marked and packed for future use. When required they can be reboiled for three minutes, and are practically as good as freshly boiled.

A Camp range
Carry a piece of sheet iron, 3ft by 2ft in which holes have been cut
for saucepans as in an ordinary range. Build three side walls with
stones to height desired (about 1ft) and place iron on top. Build fire
underneath.

Similarly concrete were the "Laundry Notes", where one learned that
"in East Africa it is unwise to dry clothes on grass or bushes, on account
of harmful insects which lay their eggs on the clothing. Should clothes
require to be bleached they must be boiled after bleaching." To avoid
having to go many miles to the dry cleaner, "it is a good habit to go over
your wardrobe and lightly sponge the heavier clothes with a little
ammonia and warm water, finishing off with a warm iron, at least once
a fortnight. In this way, spots and stains are discovered before it is too
late to deal with them at home." There were instructions for making
soap and for:

Soap saving
Tell the native servants to return the remains of old pieces of soap
when a new piece is required. Collect the old scraps for a few
weeks, then chop them or shred thinly and put in an empty tin with
cold water. Place the tin on the stove and leave till the soap is dis-
solved. When cold this sets into a jelly, and can be used in the
kitchen, for scrubbing tables, floors etc. Scraps of white soap
should be kept separate from the blue soap as the white soap jelly
is useful for washing woollens and fine articles. Scented and
coloured soaps should not be used for this purpose.

Gardening hints, tips on looking after furniture and cleaning everything imaginable, with outlines of how to make war on cockroaches,
houseflies and ants, were thrown in in case the sins of idleness should
loom. Under "Economical" we found the astounding news that "Silk
stockings that are laddered beyond repair make an excellent medium
for knitting floor rugs. Start cutting from the top of the leg round and
round the stocking until the heel is reached. Wind into balls after
sewing pieces together." "Miscellaneous" contained the charmingly
maternal "Three Hints to Bachelors": see that your bedlinen and clothes
are aired after ironing, because "many an illness has been traced to
carelessness in this matter"; how to wash your socks; and "avoid chill

as you would poison. If you come in wet, have a hot bath at once, then put on dry clothing, and take five grains of quinine, with a hot drink, preferably tea or coffee. Unless you can sit by a fire, go to bed and keep warm." The "General Rules for Washing Day" begin with advice: "It is very necessary in Kenya personally to supervise the sorting out of clothes for a washing, as boys have not the knowledge that maids at Home possess in this connexion."

"Poultry Notes" warned against Kikuyu Disease, "usually brought in through dealing with natives, and introducing among your fowls their shenzi birds". Shenzi, meaning worthless, low-grade, no good, had a multitude of uses in East Africa.

An extensive "Swahili Section" not only translated English words into Ki-Swahili but also gave phrases judged useful in English, Ki-Swahili, and the more common Ki-Settler (in Uganda, far from the Coast, after English the next and grossly inadequate *lingua franca* was a debased form of Swahili even more shenzi than Ki-Settler, called Kitchen Swahili). The 142 "Orders to Servants" caught the atmosphere of misunderstanding perfectly. "I told you to do it like this... but you do it like this" could be interpreted as exasperation or patience, or as the more common mixture of the two. With "Answer me when I speak to you," things have become a little tense. The phrase for "Be quiet" was given again under "Do not make so much noise" as translation blurred subtleties. A cri-de-coeur from the careful housewife: "Wash your hands," is followed, economy in mind, with, "Return the soap which is left". Stern, indeed oppressive, contract appears in "You are free every day from two o'clock until four o'clock, but at any other time you must be on duty on the premises". To Africans, generally required by their ancient survival customs to be courteous and hospitable, it must have seemed to be going a bit far when the bwana or memsahib said, "No-one is allowed to come here and sleep in your hut unless I give him written permission to stay". We enjoyed the ludicrous but typically British formality of "written permission". Although the book was published long before the Emergency, Mau-Mau's sinister shadow falls over items 139 to 142: "I do not allow strange boys near the house"; "Do not be sulky"; "You are insolent! You must look pleasant (or) pleased". And then, perhaps somewhat conciliatorily: "It is better not to be sulky".

The most interesting thing of all about this fascinating book, with its echoes of the domestic talk of long ago, is that it was compiled and published by the Church of Scotland Woman's Guild of St Andrew's,

Nairobi, which also revised each edition. In his foreword to the eleventh edition their breezy clergyman claimed that his church-women had "done a very great service to the domestic life of settlers in Africa as well as to St Andrew's Church". This book, then, had been produced not by toughs and bullies but by kindly, practical, Christian Scots, frontierswomen, the sort who set up schools on their farms and cared for their staff's health, the sort whom my wife had met in Germany in 1946 during her lecture tour to the occupation troops, where such women were doing outstandingly sensible work in the Church of Scotland's Mission to the Forces. What they were reflecting in East Africa, unsentimentally and truthfully, was a domestic meeting of hugely different cultures. When Europeans had begun to live and work in East Africa, a mere 40 or so years before the cookery book was first published:

> The African was frequently at the point of starvation, he was from time to time in danger of being killed or abducted by his enemies, he was almost always in a state of bodily discomfort owing to one kind or another of parasitical infection, he lived in constant fear of supernatural forces and of those he believed could influence them, and he probably had little chance of surviving beyond what is now regarded as middle age. His environment was harsh, the tools which he possessed to tame it were primitive in the extreme, and it demanded an integrated effort of a whole community to survive.

As the East Africa Royal Commission Report of 1955 pointed out, for a great number of Africans, change from a primitive society, organised around the struggle to survive, to participation as individuals in a cash economy had been, even by the fifties, almost imperceptible. To take in this light the "Orders to Servants" in the cookery book, to read them in a tone of voice that is a down-to-earth Church of Scotland woman's version of "firm but kind", is to get a domestic flavour of great difficulties and slow achievements. Even at paradisial Makerere, conditions in the halls of residence made the point: to select a homely example, such was the breakage of water glasses in the kitchens that toughened Duralex tumblers had to be ordered from France: that reduced by a little the wastage.

One imagines all the more clearly, too, the feelings of the comparatively few Africans who had risen far above the level of peasant or domestic servant but who suffered consequently a double embarrass-ment. The higher they reached the more need had they to employ African servants of their own and face the resulting domestic problems that the Church of Scotland women had been trying to help with. At the same time they had to associate with Europeans whose domestic life led them, unless they were particularly sensitive and extremely careful, to see Africans only as they most commonly were, in lowly jobs. These trials made for a difficult life for rising Africans, particularly when added to the fact that their less fortunate relations, usually a wide circle, expected to benefit materially from their success. In the special case of Buganda, Africans' tradition of fawning on superiors while exploiting inferiors showed no sign of dying fast. Servants employed by privileged Baganda were often rendered servile, fearful, incompetent and confused by their masters' disorganised mode of domestic life, a mode that could have benefited greatly from house-cleaning by those sensible Scottish women.

One thing the cookery book could not be accused of was sophisti-cation in its advertising. Typical was a full-page that asserted ambigu-ously that "Elliott's Bread, Cakes and Biscuits are the products of half a century's baking in East Africa". The most intriguing advertisements, however, were the one-liners at the top and bottom of most pages, spaces that had been bought by four companies: Ford ("Auto suggestion – FORD" and "FORD – best for the long run"); Gailey and Roberts Ltd (prosaic offerings of electric toasters, kettles, etc); Unga Ltd (various ingredients for baking bath buns, orange flan, gingerbread and so on – we always used its flour); and Woolworths. This last company's copy-writer exhausted his ingenuity by listing, page after page, all the items his firm offered: "Khaki clothing to fit you is at Woolworths" followed "Stick it with Seccotine from Woolworths" or "Pen-knives are sold by Woolworths" or "Gramophone needles" and numerous other things ditto. The inventory presumably complete at last, and he now at his wits' end but with a final slot to fill, he took refuge in the grandiloquent but ungrammatical "Woolworths stock everything".

Chapter 5   Ceremonial Occasions

Ordeal by Garden Party

To reside anywhere in East Africa was to live in mortal danger, in fear
and trembling. For at any moment there might arrive from the
Governor an invitation to one of his garden parties. To be within strike
of another territory's Governor at a relevant date put one in double
jeopardy. Church, military and university dignitaries contributed their
own variants of this hazard, as did even presidents of clubs. We
managed to confine our obligations to Uganda. Garden parties, properly,
you may protest, are delightful, informal, summery occasions of straw-
berries and cream. By so insisting you merely display your unfamiliarity
with the colonial variety, which contrived to confine informality safely
within a formal set of conventions. These invariable rules may be stated
succinctly. First, always hold the Governor's garden party in, no
surprise, the garden of Government House, regardless of the fact that
this meant out in the staggering, afternoon heat of brilliant, equatorial
sunshine. Second, require men to wear dark suits even though the only
tolerably cool tropical wear was light-coloured. Thus men had to fall
back on a dark suit made for the British climate and brought out especially for such charmingly informal tortures, the wool now magically
transformed by the heat into the thickest imaginable, no matter how
lightweight it had seemed in London. Third, ladies must wear hats and
gloves. An egregious administrator at Makerere once put out a memo-
randum reminding ladies to wear gloves, thus insulting all by assuming
that some might not. Fourth, require all guests on arrival to file past a

reception line of the Governor, his wife, his aides and possibly others, thus setting the conversational tone at desultory and making it more difficult for some to say anything spontaneous when the Governor's party eventually circulated. Fifth, throw in, normally, a military band so as not to put too heavy a demand on musical taste.

Of these fiendish trials the least bearable were those that guaranteed gallons of male sweat. Already at the start one had a wet back, clinging shirt and trouser waistband soaked as a result of driving the twenty miles from Kampala to Entebbe in the afternoon heat. To compound this aqueous condition, this feeling of being about to melt away, one had to put on one's jacket. It would have been unthinkable not to wear it and a tie. Then one presented oneself with a smiling mask of enthusiasm to be greeted. Women, of course, exulted in their flimsy frocks. One man was at least able to stay cool about his ankles. A renowned chaplain at Makerere, Fred Welbourn (who always sounded each t in "pretty" separately, like an Italian), a most charitable Anglican expert on African Christian sects, exhibited his unconventionality by never wearing socks and seeing no reason to change his habit for a mere Governor.

There were compensations. During their stint in Government House the Cohens (he was Governor when we arrived in Uganda) saw to it that the guest list was multi-racial. I do not know what it was like before their time; under their successors, the Crawfords, there were embarrassments, for Lady Crawford, who liked to play one of the Dolly Sisters in amateur musical theatricals, was said to be afflicted with a peculiarly inappropriate malady: she could not bring herself to shake hands with Africans. A charming Luo couple from Kenya, Simeon and Mary Ominde, colleagues and friends of ours at Makerere, were deeply offended when she failed to do so with them. Normally not ones to gossip, they told us that when she lived in Kenya she had refused to employ any but European chauffeurs.

The Cohens, however, welcomed African dignitaries, who came in their kanzus with a European jacket on top. It was on such an occasion that we first began to know the Kabaka's father-in-law, Mr Kisosonkole, a courtly Muganda who had married a woman from South Africa. If Baganda wives came at all they would wear their brightly patterned missionary-style dresses with the bustle. Younger African women put on European frocks and looked less splendid. Hatless Asians in their gaily-coloured silk saris were cooler than anyone else. Officers sweated in uniform, bishops in their black and purple. God may not have been in his heaven for the afternoon and all was certainly not right with the world but the band of the King's African Rifles could be relied upon to play the expected pieces with cheerful obviousness. The Union Jack, all the while, stirred dutifully in the light breeze from Victoria Nyanza.

Some of the European women from Kampala and even a few from Makerere distinguished themselves by the verve, the confection, the fantasy of their hats. This was the most delightful of the compensations offered by garden parties. It had come to be thus because an Austrian mechanic had set up shop to sell and service motor bikes. Such a mystery required investigation. We discovered the unpredictable by going into Kampala, entering the mechanic's dark, nondescript premises and picking our way through to the back of his workshop past a row of shiny, new motor bikes on each side, with others in the middle not yet assembled. Sceptically we climbed a shabby flight of stairs to the first floor, leaving below the smell of grease and oil. There, up in a long and surprisingly spacious workroom of her own, in a different world, among polished mahogany display cabinets, we found Mrs Frank, the mechanic's lively, petite wife, a Viennese milliner. How they had ended up in Kampala, after what travels and privations, nobody was ever able to discover. Even their name eluded us for a long time: there was never an invoice, we always paid cash. And how had such disparate objects as motorbikes and delightful hats come to be married? For here was a milliner who studied each customer's skull and face, how she stood and walked, what her temperament was, and made her a hat that would transform her into her loveliest self-confidence. To this genius she added a second, a marvellous sense of colour. That she had been transported (by chance? by divine dispensation, surely? riding pillion?) to this distant land of tropical garden parties was what she must have needed for fulfilment. If Aristotle said that happiness lies in the full use of one's talents, or something to that effect, we had there in Kampala a most serendipitously Aristotelian milliner. With her frivolous little clusters of gleaming black, red or yellow cherries (they looked, preposterously in the tropics, freshly picked), her swirls of muslin, here a touch of lace or subtle turn of straw, she connected us with the elegance of another empire and even managed to console us through the ordeal of being boiled alive in the Governor's garden. At one party there we saw a deceptively simple cloche, just asymmetrical enough to flatter its wearer's face, with two or three shining cherries falling casually over the little brim on one side. Beneath me, proclaimed this hat, I create a beautiful woman. My wife preferred for herself an aesthetically more severe frivolity. One of hers, an evocatively simple pink muslin and straw, seemed to derive from Fragonard. If it is true that Villon asked, "But where are the hats of yesteryear?" our Viennese milliner had her answers ready. Was it surprising, then, that each time we returned to England my wife insisted that whatever else was left behind, she must travel with her hatbox?

For those who liked royal visits, that is, despite all pretence, everyone, the Governor's garden parties were an excellent way to enjoy them. On a scale so much more intimate than the grand and crowded affairs at Buckingham Palace, where a thousand guests surge back and forth like the incoming tide and ambulances stand by to succour the trampled, the Governor's remained domestic occasions. When the young Queen and the Duke of Edinburgh came to Entebbe in 1954 the Cohens lived up to expectations. We found ourselves driving down to Government House in the usual sweat. Once there, everything at first went as usual save that all were received by a proxy Governor. The real one and his wife, we assumed, were occupied in offering tea and cake to the monarch and her consort.

At a certain point we were asked to form an oval which, with all the guests around, was large but by no means overwhelming. The royal couple, looking relaxed and cheerful, then came out of the house with the Cohens. The Queen stayed at that end of the oval and moved about talking to people there. The Duke sauntered towards the other end. Some of us had been selected as his possible targets, so that with his aide's help he could fix upon a few to talk to. He bore down upon us, smiling as though to say that if he had to do this he was going to enjoy it. Standing close next to me was one of the professors, a man of about fifty, distinguished in his field, self-important rather than pompous, yet vulnerable and so self-conscious that he blushed easily. The Duke now stood directly before us, a young man of my own age. His aide whispered something to him, whereupon he addressed to the professor a breezy, naval question so deflating, given the recipient, that it seemed to have been especially designed to discomfit him: "And what's your racket?"

Not a word came from my neighbour. He was blushing a particularly startling colour, something between puce and magenta. Such was the beneficent power of a royal presence that all to be heard was a rumbling from deep in his throat, an unintelligible, strangled utterance suggestive of earliest man's first effort at speech. The Duke again, amused: "Well, what do you do?"

In answer to this mercifully orthodox way of putting it my poor neighbour managed to mutter that he was the professor of his subject, information that the Duke no doubt had just received from his aide.

"Pretty important stuff," said the Duke, then moved on in search of action elsewhere, leaving my neighbour mortified but already struggling to put back his devastated self into a persona that he could live with. The power of royal words, as this encounter showed, was enormous. That the eagerness to receive them, whatever they might be, was ardent, consuming, destructive of all the customary facades of social composure was illustrated when, on a later occasion, the Queen Mother came to Makerere to open the new library. Politicking for the honour of being among the few to be presented was ingenious and cut-throat. The administration, immobilised for weeks by claim and counterclaim, made plans, scrapped them, and re-drafted. When at last the great day came the Queen Mother beamed impartially upon us all and as though with a sigh of satisfaction everyone claimed success.

Bonnie King Freddie

In 1953 among Europeans in Uganda there was much talk of the economic advances expected as a result of electrification flowing west-wards from the newly-constructed Jinja dam across the Nile. Among Africans there was no such optimism, for the Baganda in particular harboured suspicions of European "development": to them it smacked too much of a plot to destroy Africans' traditions and reduce their power. On the other hand, in one way or another all races at that time were interested in the dramatic political events unfolding in Buganda. Before an account of further ceremonial occasions we must digress into the course of those events and meet the people most involved.

Only four years before we arrived, serious riots had broken out in Buganda. These were mainly protests against the upper crust of the Baganda by the less well-off, but arson and looting had spread to include much Asian property too. A protectorate official had been hit on the head by a brick while trying to read the Riot Act one sunny day. More happily, a detachment of the King's African Rifles, brought over from Kenya to help control the rioters, had contributed greatly to public order by its popular band concerts.

The memory of these disturbances, together with fears caused by the Mau-Mau rebellion in Kenya, had left the Protectorate Government staff at Entebbe and out in the districts understandably jumpy. The Governor and Commander-in-Chief of Uganda when we arrived, Andrew Cohen, had been formerly a senior official in the Colonial Office and was thus an unusual appointment to a governorship. Known as a liberal, he supported "progressive" policies such as the development of African marketing co-operatives, the improvement of African education, the supposed democratisation of the Buganda constitution and rapid movement towards a united, independent Uganda. In support of these causes he provided funds from his large reserve and moved about the country to speak and show himself. His imposing size and a face forbidding in repose gave a misleading impression of toughness, contradicting his reputation. Decisive and resolute he could certainly be but in conversation I found him a shy and gentle man, diffident, kindly, and occasionally tongue-tied. When I thanked him once for making some supportive comments in a speech he retreated into the self-deprecating defence that one got into the habit of repeating the same sorts of thing. I was to find him particularly considerate and helpful in 1956 when Makerere was embarrassed by a strange request from the representative in East Africa of the International Confederation of Free Trade Unions (ICFTU).

At ridiculously short notice the ICFTU had decided to set up in Kampala an international college for trade unionists and to bring in students from around the world. It had no premises, no staff or syllabus, no materials for study. Could Makerere please help, its representative pleaded. I replied that, immediately, we could not: we were already fully committed to our normal work. If the ICFTU could produce specific and detailed proposals we should consider each one on its merits, as we should any specific request for help from a responsible body. I informed the Uganda Labour Commissioner, who was grateful but not perturbed. Hitherto he had heard nothing of this bizarre proposal; he undertook to write to the other territories.

I found relations with all the Labour Commissioners, as with many more junior officers, pleasantly easy and productive. The three East African Governments, however, were much concerned at what they considered potentially subversive action behind their backs by the

ICFTU, action that seemed to threaten them with the importation of foreign "agitators". Some senior officials let their view be known that Makerere should have told the ICFTU flatly that in no circumstances could the college help it. Andrew Cohen took the trouble to have a private talk with me, during which he showed himself sensitive to the college's embarrassment at receiving such an ill-considered request from a world body. He quickly grasped the details, agreed that we could not have given an absolute refusal, and offered to tell the other governors that. Nevertheless the Kenya Government, suspicious of the ICFTU representative's motives because convinced that he was a communist, got in touch with Vincent Tewson, General Secretary of the Trades Union Congress in London, to request his help in having the man recalled. Whether at Tewson's behest or by some other machination in the ICFTU's arcane politics, the Kenya Government's wish was granted. Of the grandiose but empty scheme for an international trade union college in Kampala we heard no more.

It was incongruous and unfortunate that it should have been during Cohen's governorship that the Protectorate Government withdrew recognition from Kabaka (King) Mutesa II of Buganda and packed him off to England towards the end of 1953. The row had arisen over the Kabaka's publicly stated objections to Britain's alleged intention to federate the East African territories and to Cohen's evident support of Uganda as a unitary state, policies which the Kabaka and most other Baganda saw as a threat to Buganda's separateness and separatism. With the charming contrariness of politics, no sooner was their king exiled than those Baganda who had previously quarreled over his political powers and objected to his untraditionally licentious behaviour began to close ranks in condemnation of the Governor's "high-handedness".

Expression of hatred for Europeans was widely heard among the Baganda. Quickly they developed an unusual solidarity among themselves and increased hostility towards immigrant ("foreign") tribes. Many let their beards grow in mourning for their absent, divine monarch. They collected money for the campaign for his return. Five days of public lamentation were proclaimed.

At Makerere, naturally, Europeans and Africans discussed these dramatic developments endlessly. Tony Low's substantial and informed despatches appeared in *The Times*. In the *Uganda Argus* the editor, Mark Barrington-Ward, showed himself much exercised about the crisis. Meanwhile Kabaka Mutesa, known generally as "the Kabaka" or more familiarly as "Freddie", was enjoying himself in London on a British Government allowance. There he was reported to be perfectly happy to stay: his honorary membership of a Guards regiment, his elegantly cut suits, his perfect shoes and Cambridge accent to go with them opened fashionable doors to him and his current concubine, his official wife's sister. About her exact status puzzled questions were asked at Buckingham Palace.

No matter how much his Bishop, back in Uganda, might raise his eyebrows and grievingly shake his head, as I saw him do at dinner when he had just been confronted with news of the supposedly Christian Kabaka's lapse into spectacular adultery, that monarch rested at ease with the hallowed perquisites of his own divine responsibilities. By indulging in lustful concubinage he was doing no more than supporting a tradition enthusiastically kept alive by his male subjects. Save in one respect: while it was admirable to the Baganda for a man to sleep with his "ring wife's" sister(s) as well as with such other women as he chose, it profoundly offended totem-clan sensibilities if he did so with her elder sister. The beauty in the London bedroom was undeniably such a forbidden person. When their affair started, in Uganda, the Baganda, aghast at their monarch's affront to the nation's prospects (for clan-offensive misdeeds at the highest, divine level could lead, they knew, only to the whole people's downfall), had begun to talk of deposing him in favour of someone less of a libertine by their standards. To be exiled to London had saved him. The Baganda's deep unease shifted to a surrogate cause: Governor replaced Kabaka as the focus for outrage and hostility.

During all this time the tension in Buganda ran high. Riots were confidently expected but none occurred on the scale of 1949. Crowds gathered here and there and milled about. Europeans prudently stayed away from them; nobody was hurt. The incidence of arson remained normal. Out on peaceful Makerere Hill, however, the Academic Board (potent, grave and reverend signiors all) assembled to discuss what to do if serious rioting were to start. Someone proposed that in such a case all members of staff and their families should gather for shelter and defence in the Administration Building. This they had done for a night in 1949, together with the then small number of students: on that night one house on the Hill had been burnt down. Although no vote was taken the proposal found favour, to judge by the doom-faced mumblings of pessimists that this time it might have to be for longer than just a night.

A very senior professor then astonished me, and I trust provided light relief to many others, by portentously suggesting that in such an emergency I should be put in charge of the building's defence. My military credentials were of course impeccable. After the war had I not lectured for a year and a half at the Royal Military Academy, Sandhurst? But that had been in political economy, a detail overlooked by the proposer of my elevation to supreme command. Still, soon after I had arrived at Makerere Cyril Ehrlich had opined in the Faculty Common Room that I looked like a cavalry officer. Could that have counted as a recommendation? True, I had served for a few weeks in the Local Defence Volunteers (later re-named the Home Guard) while waiting to go up to Oxford in 1940 but my extensive training to resist the expected invasion by elite Nazi troops had consisted of being allowed to fire one round from a French carbine that had a particularly nasty kick. On the other hand, while in that gallant force I had received an invaluable piece of military instruction from Harold Llewellyn-Smith, one of my schoolmasters, when we were on watch together for German paratroopers throughout one night: "Always aim for their balls". This he had picked up while learning his manners as a boy at Winchester. It was during that same night-watch that I was sure I had seen a German in the pre-dawn. Heroically, carbines cocked, we stationed ourselves behind a Cornish wall. As the light came up the German miraculously transformed himself into a cow.

Again, I could not deny having attained the exalted rank of Flying Officer before being invalided out but like all Royal Air Force aircrew I should have felt far safer aloft than defending anything on the ground. If one had to put aside farce, Kenneth Ingham, with his Military Cross, or Paul Vowles, with his Mention in Despatches, would have been far better able to defend us all. I asserted something about being of course ready to help in any way I was qualified for (the significance of this less clear to others than to me) and quickly added that we should do nothing to increase tension (firm "Hear hears" from Bernard de Bunsen and Kenneth Baker), that I believed such a desperate emergency plan would not be required given that we were the university, not government or shops, and that our own Baganda students showed not the least sign of rioting against us. Fortunately so it turned out: the building, long and with many entrances and windows, would not have been at all easy to defend against determined assault. As we shall see, it would have been tactlessly divisive to add that we had no weapons (a professor who had owned an arsenal by now having died) apart from an antique elephant rifle, a couple of shotguns, and the odd service revolver, probably rusted.

In 1955 the Kabaka was allowed to return from exile, now supposedly as the constitutional monarch of Buganda and loyal adherent to the protectorate agreement with Britain, but in fact with his power greatly increased by revived forces of traditional feeling. All along the 20 miles from Entebbe airport to Kampala the Baganda massed to greet him. Prostrating themselves as he passed, they welcomed him home as the father of his people: literally, said the wags. Yet how indelicately boorish one could unwittingly be if one failed to remember that. For example, take the case of the newly-arrived faculty wife whom we last met tottering into Kampala, naked by Buganda standards. For this and similar reasons she had come to the Kabaka's attention, so much so that, charmed, he invited her up to Mengo Hill. One afternoon, then, she presented herself and was soon being shown over his rambling palace by His Highness himself. In order to suggest, perhaps, that all things were possible, he took her into a house where a mother was nursing her new-born child. The visitor brightly asked the Kabaka, "And who's the lucky father of this beautiful baby?" This story she told us herself with a naivete as complex as Marilyn Monroe's, but she remained resolutely coy about what happened next or on her subsequent visits.

With the Kabaka, this popular, symbolic and actual prolific progenitor (a lazy and conceited student told me once with pride that he was "a true son of the Kabaka") about to return from exile, enthusiastic crowds of his subjects had for several weeks been renewing the woven fences around the palace and its extensive grounds. These fences, signifying the Kabaka's separateness, authority and prestige, had been allowed to grow tattered during his absence. Parts had fallen down, in fact had not been maintained properly for some time before his exile. Now the volunteer workers were excited, some frenzied. Only women were working on the fences themselves. It was their private, Buganda occasion, they all clearly felt, a matter of their own pride and traditions: Europeans or Asians were not welcome. Nevertheless, my wife decided to drive up there. As a medievalist she wanted to see for herself this authentic fence-building, marking a boundary that divided those who belonged from strangers. Fortunately she had thought to take Alisi with her. Together they left the car and penetrated quite deeply into the inner compounds, saw the internal reed fences separating various buildings and areas of the palace. They had been there for about 20 minutes (my wife said it seemed much longer) before the crowd showed signs of becoming hostile. Alisi told them something to the effect that this memsahib was a friend of the Kabaka's. To my wife she suggested with admirable calm that it might be better if they went back to the car now. This they did, unhurriedly, smiling all the time at the women. Thanks to their presence of mind I was able to hear the story at teatime and chide my intrepid wife, for violence was certainly in the air. Descriptions were coming in of Baganda savagely beaten, their kanzus soaked with blood, for being suspected of disloyalty to the Kabaka during his exile.

My own, far less adventurous, visit to Mengo in these disturbed times was to attend the ceremonial opening of the reformed Lukiko (the parliament of Buganda) on the Kabaka's return. A colleague and I were given seats in the low gallery, near the Kabaka's throne, with a full view of the proceedings. His Highness was very late; it must have been an hour or more after the announced time that the ceremony began. Meanwhile we had the leisure to examine the setting. On a dais at one end of the long room, just below us to our right, stood the Kabaka's throne, draped with a superb leopard skin. Around it were spread various sizes of Persian carpets of excellent quality, some large. Further out, layers of skins, leopard uppermost, covered the dais. In front of it more rugs and skins cushioned the floor. These layers increased in depth near the dais and directly in front of the throne so as to make a slight mound consisting of splendid lion, leopard and cheetah skins. Around the walls, away from the throne, numerous Africans stood about unprepossessingly. These we took to be the members of the Lukiko.

At last the Kabaka appeared. We all stood. A slight figure, he was wearing a simple, white robe, lightly embroidered, and looked far less at ease, patently less the carefree Freddie, than in his Savile Row suits. Now a well-built African carrying a spear came forward from the back of the hall. He was dressed in a traditional ochre bark-cloth robe fastened over one shoulder like a toga. No doubt it had been beaten out from ficus natalensis ("mutuba" in Luganda), the best of the three sorts of fig tree used for the purpose. As he neared the mound he prostrated himself, face well down, and wriggled, quivering, for several seconds. Then he got up, took a few steps forward, and repeated his abasement. By the time he reached the mound in front of the dais, after further halts, his wriggles had become more sustained. The person giving this virtuoso performance of abject fear was the Katikiro, the chief minister of Buganda. The Kabaka, as He Who Dealt Life and Death but looking as bored as Edward VIII was said to have looked on ceremonial occasions, came forward to the edge of the dais, stretched out his foot and placed it on his symbolically terrified minister's extended neck. Even though the Kabaka's power was now so much greater than his new status as constitutional monarch might suggest, this ceremonial act was no defiance of the agreements that he had signed. It was, rather, an effete, vestigial gesture, preserved in ritual from a line of quasi-divine despots who, not too long before, had had the power, and had used it daily as had their creatures the chiefs, to condemn subjects to be massacred in their hundreds or, as a concession, to be thrown to the crocodiles in the sacrificial lake nearby. With this reminder of the Buganda people's hardly joyful past the ceremony ended, leaving behind it still the memory of horrors that had caused a British official in 1894 to call Buganda "a whited sepulchre concealing the festering bones, the foulness of iniquity, and the hideous decay behind the pleasing surface".

"Why Abunwazi Went to Gaol"

Here is the third of my wife's tales.

"One day, at breakfast, Alisi came in to say that Abunwazi had not returned from Wandegeya market at the foot of the Hill, where he had gone at about eight o'clock the evening before to buy plantains and groundnuts for his supper. Abunwazi is young, new to Kampala. He comes from the western hills. Everything he can save from his wages he puts by to take back one day to his family. He doesn't drink, says very little, seems to need no company outside our other staff; leads, in fact, the sober, meticulous life of an uneducated but devout Moslem.

"Alisi thought he must be in trouble.

"'I shouldn't worry, Alisi. He has been spending the night with friends, perhaps?'

"'He knows nobody in Kampala, always comes straight back from market.'

"'He's not drunk?! Lying somewhere on the Hill?"

"'Oh no, not that, memsahib. He is a good Moslem. And I've already

72

1. ABOVE. HM the
Queen Mother
opening the Library,
1959, with Bernard
de Bunsen
(Crawfords behind).

2. RVC about to
leave for a garden
party at
Government House,
Entebbe.

3. Alisi (right) and Nyesi wearing busutis, with Abunwazi.

4. Northcote Hall's great Dining Hall, kitchens in foreground.

5. Mary Ominde, then Assistant Domestic Bursar, Northcote Hall.

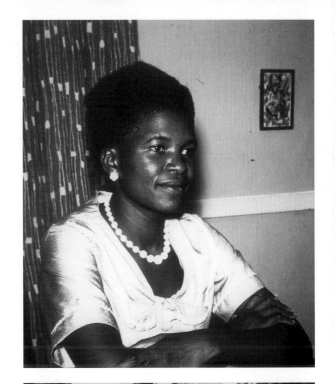

6. With African friends after tea at the garden house.

7. ABOVE. Arabs' Silent March against 1956 attack on Suez and Egypt by Britain and Israel.

8. BELOW. The Americans: Fred Hadsel and SJC on either side of Neta Jones. Ambassador Taft behind SJC.

asked around. He must have been picked up by the Kabaka's askaris.'

"'Whatever for?'

"'Ahaaah!' The long-drawn warning note in her voice.

"'Can you find out?'

"'Yes, memsahib, by midday. My brother is a carpenter in the workshops here. He will put through a call to a friend of his at Mengo. If Abunwazi has been arrested he will be up there in the Kabaka's gaol.'

"At lunch she came in to confirm that that was where he was. He must have been picked up on his way back from the market. A lorryful of the Kabaka's askaris had been out arresting any African they met on the road.

"'What do we do now?'

"'Go up to the gaol and pay the fine, please, memsahib.'

"So in the hot afternoon I drove up to Mengo Hill with Alisi, who directed me to the mud-stained, whitewashed huts clustered about the prison. She took me to the Charge Room with its beaten earth floor. Behind a wooden counter stood the duty officer, a Muganda, one of the Kabaka's askaris in crumpled khaki uniform and red fez. His bloodshot eyes probably came from heavy drinking the night before. As everyone knows, that's what the Kabaka's police get up to in the Katwe bars. In front of him lay the charge book. The sides of the room were open to the air. All around, on the dusty red soil streaked with rain-runnels, sat a crowd of curious Africans, there for the day's entertainment, no doubt, and now delighted to watch this unusual drama. The askari ordered Alisi outside with them but she stayed at the front of the crowd in order to hear, and to guide me by making appropriate noises.

"I exchanged the necessary greetings with the askari in Swahili since I was in no mood to sigh and hum my way through the long, polite Luganda salutation.

"'Where is Abunwazi?' I then asked, still in my best kitchen Swahili.

"He replied, incomprehensibly to me, in Luganda.

"'My houseboy, why is he here?' I persisted in Swahili, for I knew my Luganda lessons had not equipped me to argue the law.

"The askari shouted, in English, 'You no speak good Swahili'.

"To this angry but accurate insult I retorted, 'And you no speak good English'.

"At this exchange the crowd outside tittered, whether from amusement or embarrassment I could not tell because the Baganda titter in either case.

73

"I tapped the charge book.

"'Why is Abunwazi in gaol?'

"Alisi tut-tutted a warning that I was going too far. She whispered urgently and to the point, 'Ask him how much, memsahib.'

"The askari pursed his lips and severely ignored the growing crowd. But he did grudgingly show me the charge book. There was the entry at the bottom of the page. He stubbed his forefinger at Abunwazi's name as though the mere fact of its being there proved the charge, Kwe tambulare, which sounded to me mystifyingly like Latin.

"'Just for walking about!' I exploded.

"He said it meant walking without a lantern after curfew.

"'But,' I protested, 'the Kabaka's curfew is not until nine o'clock. And in any case Abunwazi was on the Queen's highway, not the Kabaka's.'

"Alisi tut-tutted again at this imprudent sally and even more urgently pleaded with me to ask him what the fine was.

"'How much?' in my elementary Luganda.

"'Shillingi ten.' He managed to smile now.

"I opened my handbag and paid the fine. The askari picked up a key, went out, and soon returned with Abunwazi. The poor lad looked stunned and hungry.

"'Let's get away, memsahib,' Alisi called out. The crowd was silent as we three walked to the car. On the way home she told me that if they had picked up a woman they would have said she could afford to pay a 70 shilling fine, for only prostitutes would be out so late.

"Later I telephoned to the Protectorate Attorney General to tell him this terrible tale of the miscarriage of justice and ask his advice on what to do next.

"'Drop it,' he said.

"'Why drop it? What are we here for if not to keep law and order?'

"'If you value your houseboy's life, don't pursue it further.'

"Not long afterwards I was chatting at a party with Mr Maini, the Asian minister in the Protectorate Government. He told me that this was how the Buganda police always raised money for the Kabaka's birthday reception."

I received an invitation to that reception, and went, there to chat with the urbane King Freddie, whose superb suit gave him far and away the most elegantly draped back in East Africa.

Chapter 6   Wildlife and Diseases

Visitors came to East Africa longing to see the wildlife. In contrast, our proper study, vile man, most thought less worthy of attention. Not all, however: a beaky, stiffly-walking, severely kind headmaster, retired from public schools, did think to ask me, "Is it true about African penises?" Certainly there were wonderful game parks but in some of these, even with game abundant, we found a disappointingly artificial atmosphere. When we saw, in the Nairobi Park, a score of crowded cars converging on a patch of long grass for occasional glimpses of a few sleepy, disdainful lion heads, it was as though even in the fifties modern man, by sitting and staring, was intruding with shameless vulgarity where he did not belong. In the larger and wilder reserves, Amboseli or Serengeti, it was no different fundamentally. Tourists went out in vehicles to spy on game ignobly, had to impose themselves incongruously, the days of walking among the beasts not yet past but by now confined to small parties of serious hunters, game wardens or, occasionally, devoted researchers. By living in East Africa we came to accept that the wildlife was all around us, all the time. While driving from Kampala to Nairobi, say, setting about one's business and keeping to the road, whatever one glimpsed in the bush along the way was observed but not intruded upon, whether it was a man leading a file of mud-smeared boys going through their initiation ceremonies, or a group of animals. We accepted that the whole country was wild. Even in the towns and cities the abundant fauna were overwhelmingly present, successfully destroying the illusion that East African urban life was sanitised and safe.

Had we been settlers in Kenya we might have had some of the experiences that Mirella Ricciardi (see biographical index) and others have described. Tiny dik-dik would no doubt have nibbled our flowers in the garden at night. From time to time a leopard might have crouched on the roof, in wait in the dark, while warthogs snorted in the rough. Locusts would surely have crowded in to stop for a day or two to eat all greenery within sight before rushing off to pay their compliments to other unfortunates. On our hill in the municipality of Kampala, however, we had our own excitements. Take the joy of cockroaches. In spite of initial reluctance, fairmindedness requires one to admit that these under-appreciated creatures are as much part of nature as cheetahs or elephants. Their venerable age in the history of species and their excellent chance of outlasting mankind should convince us of their claim to respect. Until, that is, they get into the milk. How they managed to do so we could never decide. Alisi made for us some small, circular, embroidered cloths with beads around the edge. These were designed to cover milk jugs in particular. She would pour milk from a tetrapak, cover the jug immediately with one of these cloths, and put it in the refrigerator. When she made tea for early morning or afternoon she brought the jug in on the tray, or out into the garden, its cloth still undisturbed. Our first act was to lift the cloth cautiously and, as we became used to East Africa, expectantly. Occasionally we were disappointed but frequently enough to justify odds there was a cockroach swimming in our milk. Curiosity was submerged for a moment in disgust as we spooned the athlete out and dispatched him but questions soon resurfaced.

How had he got in? Had he lurked in the refrigerator, impervious to cold? If he had, were all his relations still there? Or when Alisi's back was turned had he sneaked from behind something on the kitchen counter and dived into the milk via some small fold in the cloth? Certainly the East African cockroach was capable of squeezing itself into the minutest crack. Few things were more infuriating than to charge off in full pursuit of one, only to find it disappearing into a space where only an ant could hope to follow. This feat was all the more astonishing because of the size of these cockroaches. Young ones were of course small, dear, lovable little babies worthy of being adored by any rock star, but adults were up to two brown inches long. They could fly as well as scurry; they could and did squeal when cornered; tirelessly and ubiquitously they were about at any time of the day or night cunningly laying their ornately packaged eggs. Anything at all was likely to have a cockroach under, in or behind it, although it must be said that their particular prank was to hide in shoes or trouser legs, or inside frocks and hats. It was pointless to try to exterminate them by fumigation. A few of those in the house might by this unheroic means be killed but a fresh abundance of immigrants would immediately move in from the garden.

One of their more endearing characteristics was a love of books. Something in the hard covers, delicious glue no doubt, gave them such delirious pleasure that they could not resist nibbling trails across them. There could be no question of peace with such invaders: even though victory was unattainable, relentless guerrilla warfare was the only honourable course. This noble clash of species brought forth its heroes. One night at dinner in hall, with students and faculty all very formal in their gowns, the waiters placed on high table the usual battered aluminium bowls containing vegetables. As soon as one of the lids was removed a very large cockroach, the Hector of his kind, jumped down and wandered nonchalantly along the polished table. Conversation ceased in respect for such bravado. Then someone flicked at the creature with a fork, the cockroach made a dash, and another diner, with amazing dexterity, caught it in his hand. But what to do with it? Calmly he squashed it between his fingers, dropped the remains to the floor, wiped the nauseating, creamy white fluid from his hands with his napkin, and proceeded deliberately with his dinner. A champion's triumph, but others present seemed to have lost their appetite.

Mosquitoes were not disgusting, simply exceedingly dangerous. For fear of malaria, no sensible household would fail to close its window screens well before dark. Always a houseboy would go round every room at dusk to pump his flitgun behind chairs, under sofas or beds, in the air. Yet frequently at dinner we would be buzzed by one that had escaped the spray or got in by the back door. Every night we expected to be woken up by the high-pitched whine as one of them circled the face in search of a tender spot. To slap a mosquito as it settled to bite and see the splash of blood raised the uneasy question whether it was one's own or someone else's. Termites, on the other hand, deserved attention for quite different reasons. They had created a feature of the landscape with their numerous, enormous, rock-hard, red anthills that stood up in emphatic, anarchic mockery of phallic man's impermanence. They also contributed an essential element of Buganda's characteristic smell, an acrid, pervasive suggestion of sweat. Termites liked to eat away the wooden parts of buildings; they marked concrete or stuccoed walls with the red veins of their travels to target. More helpful to man, at times they provided food. Sometimes at night we would hear an excited hullabaloo and see a cloud of termites flying up to a roadlamp. Africans appeared at first to be leaping, clapping, urging them up. Closer inspection revealed that they were catching the termites, rubbing the wings off quickly between their hands, and eating the disabled but still wriggling insects immediately. One intrepid (or gullible?) colleague told us that they tasted like raspberry jam. We could never work up enough enthusiasm to join in the fun and find out. Africans would also roast them and offer them for sale in the market.

No visitor could fail to like the tiny, transparent lizards, geckoes, that ran up and down the walls of every house, indoors and out, their hearts visibly palpitating. Too alert and agile to be caught, harmless to humans, they slept goodness knows where and lived on insects. Such useful inoffensiveness tended to restore belief in the beneficence of Providence when so much else was maleficent. Similarly restorative were the creatures that simply appeared and put their trust in our benevolence. At tea in the garden one day, as we sat in our cool basket chairs, a head peered round the hedge. It withdrew, then reappeared and continued to watch us. In time, part of a body followed the head. It was a large Siamese tom. I stood up; he retreated. I sat; his head tentatively reappeared. So tactful and wary a request for help could not be ignored. I put a saucer of milk at the end of the hedge. By this time he was a watchful way away. When I sat down again he materialised and drank. Eventually we stood up; he left. Next day, however, he was back and the introduction was extended. We put out some food as well as the saucer. That decided him, for he allowed us to stroke him, then came hesitantly into the house. This magnificent cat, his cream flanks always beautifully clean, had come to stay with us. Nobody claimed him. Presumably he had once belonged to people who had left. Perhaps he had walked all the way out from Kampala, or been stolen then abandoned.

Whatever his provenance, he was the most delightful, tactful, intelligent cat imaginable, even gently tolerant of children. A couple of years later, when the time came to start to pack our belongings to leave East Africa, our beautiful guest disappeared. Anxiously we waited through the days for his return: he was nowhere on the Hill. When we had to leave, Victor Ford offered to look out for him but it was all too clear that the cat had understood what was happening and had set off in search of a new home. I miss him still. Another stray adopted us for a much shorter time, no more than ten days. A splendid young Alsatian, good-tempered and in excellent condition, bounced in and made himself comfortable on the bearskin. A few days later he distinguished himself by pulling our Christmas dinner from a serving shelf on to the concrete floor and shattering the dish. Not long afterwards his Asian owner, who had advertised his loss in a newspaper, came from Kampala to claim him. Since most Asians, naturally, did not celebrate Christmas, the dog was sensibly seizing a once-only chance.

Heartless purists will protest that dogs and cats are too internationally domesticated truly to count as East African fauna. What about the great cats, the big game that everyone wants to spy on? These creatures, too, were all about us in one sense or another. The *Uganda Argus*, for example, reported one day that there were hopes in Western Uganda of hunting down a lion that had broken into a hut and fatally mauled an African. In Kenya and Tanganyika, parties of young Masai, those inveterate cattle-thieves, still went out in search of a lion to encircle and enrage so that it could be goaded into trying to break out from the ring. The drill then was that whoever took the beast's charge on his shield must stand his ground.

For the intrepid visitor to Uganda, sickened by the gawping, sedentary carloads in the gameparks yet not quite up to Masai standards, there was always the possibility of taking the Lake steamer down to Mwanza, then making the slow journey by dusty train from there 200 miles further south into Tanganyika to the formerly German town of Tabora (before that the inland centre of the slave trade), where he would enjoy an excellent chance of being eaten by one of the many lions that liked to stroll through the town. Or if such amusement were insufficiently distracting, he might consider driving out to the hot plains of Ankole, in south-western Uganda, and asking politely to put up for a while in a Bahima herdsman's boma, a few huts inside a hedge of thorn or prickly euphorbia. There he could wait in company with the magnificently long-horned Ankole cattle to see if such a hedge really did keep out lions, as it was reputed and intended to in this lion country, where the cattle habitually stood together in a tight bunch for fear of their marauding enemy.

Snakes, of course, had to be watched for even in what might seem the most unlikely places. A driver in the formidable East African safari race stopped his car by the side of the road miles from anywhere, got out to relieve himself, was bitten by a snake as he did so and died there shortly afterwards. One did not have to go as far as he to see snakes. On the road to Kenya I was forced to a complete stop by a most unusual sight. A large, stationary python had stretched himself out across the road, strangely abandoned behaviour for a creature normally so shy. A bump roughly in his middle (he must have been more than 20 feet long) suggested that he had distended his jaws for no mere tit-bit and was now enjoying an after-lunch nap. With deep ditches on each side of the road I had no choice but to wake the poor fellow up by sounding the hooter. He may have been slow-witted or old and deaf, but at last it penetrated that there was an unpleasant noise and he slowly moved off. Back at Makerere a few condemned me for not having run him over. They, of course, had not witnessed his substantial girth, but I could claim neither prudence nor fine feelings. I had simply been too fascinated to feel murderous.

Chance encounters with wild creatures by no means always turned out as peacefully. Some human beings might show compunction about killing animals, but certain animals did not reciprocate. A settler acquaintance in Kenya told us of elderly friends of his who were out walking, unarmed, on their farm one evening. Suddenly in front of them, and close by, stood a rhinoceros. The farmer pushed his wife back out of the way while he tried to frighten off the huge beast. Unimpressed and bad-tempered, the rhinoceros charged, knocked him down, and ripped him with its horn. The woman, fleeing, looked back to see the animal furiously trampling her husband's corpse. Yet in another violent case it was man who was victorious. Legendary was the courage of an unarmed African game warden who was attacked by a leopard while walking home from work. The dangerous animal bit and clawed as they rolled over, but so did the man, to such effect that although badly mauled himself he killed his adversary. Then he walked the rest of the way home. An official report fully recorded his exploit; with typically British interest in a fair fight, it described him as a small man, not greatly different in weight from the leopard.

Children, of course, were much more at risk. Shortly before we arrived in East Africa the District Commissioner at Ruponda, in the Southern Province of Tanganyika, stated in his annual report that numbers of baboons had been shot to protect crops. As a result, leopards were going hungry and had taken 14 children. Lions, too, had turned their talents to mankilling in other parts of the Southern Province. During the fighting between the German forces and the Allies in German East Africa (Tanganyika) in the Great War, bees and rhinos as well as lions had interrupted battles and frequently proved more of a menace to the troops on each side than the enemy soldiers.

Fortunately our own encounters with wild animals away from the game parks were not at all hand to claw. While returning from Kenya to Uganda, with the children and Nyesi in the car, we came upon a small group of giraffe elegantly browsing on the high branches a few yards from the road. It was a quiet, almost domestic scene, and we stopped to watch them. One, a female, stayed behind the others as they moved sedately along. She looked abstracted, then spread her rear legs and began to urinate. What started as an impressive cascade continued as a substantial waterfall, and continued... until we were all overcome with laughter at such a generous evacuation. "Look, she hasn't finished yet," cried the children.

When at last she wandered off we were left to wonder at what must be the immense capacity of a giraffe's bladder. Was it possible that these disdainful creatures urinated only once a month and had within themselves elongated cavities for storage?

On another occasion I left Nairobi alone before dawn, hoping to drive all the way to Kampala that day. As the light came up I was passing Lake Naivasha, the road empty. There on the great open stretch to my left, as the land declined gently to the lake, I saw herds of zebra grazing, and eland. If they were alert for predators they showed no sign of it. Such a peaceful moment gave me the illusion of being there not only at the dawn of day but in the beginning of human consciousness, in that Eden of our earliest upright ancestors, long before even the aboriginal age of man's first obsidian-tipped javelins. No new world, this, but our oldest homeland. So great an expanse of slope, lake and sky might have been expected to leave busy, modern man feeling superfluous as, after so many millennia of generations, he sat chilly in his car, alone with his primeval feelings in the upland, tropical first light. On the contrary, I felt strangely at home and at ease, assuaged by a sense of unity. Man's consciousness and conscience – or so my early morning thoughts ran – are not at odds with an unfeeling, unconscious universe such as terrified Pascal. The cosmos is conscious and capable of caring because we are of it, not outside it: no cause for screaming anguish from Francis Bacon's exhibitionist figures as they writhe in their entrapment, their interval between being and not-being. Yet in future eras of evolution, when we have been superseded, will anything be able to realise how poignant for each of us was our beautiful, fleeting time of awareness?

Sometimes considerably larger than usual, sometimes smaller, depending on the rains, Lake Naivasha, at 6000 feet above sea level, sheltered not only fish-eagles, pelicans and many other water and lake-edge birds but in particular thousands of flamingoes. During a holiday we drove the children down to see them. With the rainy season about to begin, a bank of indigo storm-cloud was massing to sweep across the lake. Flamingoes were everywhere. They crowded into the shallows and took off every so often to circle the lake like young pilots practising circuits and bumps. Against the threatening clouds their pink showed up delicately. We were the only people within sight to observe all this loveliness. In Uganda, some colleagues who lived off the Hill, away in the country, ensured their own supply of exotic elegance by keeping Crested Cranes in their garden, with two Great Danes to guard them. On the Hill or in the Protectorate Government gardens at Entebbe one could see delightful humming birds and other, larger flashes of colour in flight. Around the Kampala market, however, repulsively naked vultures would sit, waiting for scraps. A brief expedition into the dense, green gloom of one of the few surviving Buganda forests convinced me that my remote ancestors must have been folk who kept to the open hills, not dwellers in the "evil forest". Startling, apparently purposeless shrieks and whistles of unseen birds I found unnerving, as I did the half-light and the feeling of being unable to protect my back no matter which way I turned. Glad to escape out into the sunshine, I never again wanted to venture into the claustrophobic company of the forest birds.

Coughs and sneezes, wartime posters had proclaimed in Britain, spread diseases. Apart from some notable exceptions, when we moved to East Africa we were left uninformed about tropical diseases and how they were communicated. It had been a century of major medical advances since Burton and Speke had completed their great safari from the coast to Lake Tanganyika, a journey that had taken them seven-and-a-half months through dangerous country then unknown to Europeans. All the way they had been ill. Marsh fever had followed malaria;

nameless other fevers had led to ulcers, attacks of paralysis and near-blindness, so that at times each of these courageous explorers had had to be carried. Even during the Great War, losses of men and animals from disease among the Allied forces in East Africa had outstripped by far the number of those killed or wounded in action. It was not that these sufferings had been forgotten but that since their day the medical successes in the struggle against major killers had tended to lull Europeans into a false feeling of security. Yellow fever, typhus, cholera, tetanus we were required to be inoculated against. There were probably other ingredients, too, in the soup pumped into our arms. Malaria was too great and obvious a danger to be forgotten. Although there was no preventive, our instructions were to begin taking a suppressant, Daraprim tablets, before we went out from England and to keep it up. Later we were told to switch to Paludrine to keep the malaria organisms guessing.

Nevertheless, when we arrived at Makerere it did not occur to us that on and around this summery estate there lay in wait numerous other invisible fauna, some merely unpleasant, others lethal. Even our early dysentery, too easily explicable as an adjustment sickness, failed to alert us to the dangers. Gradually we learned that we had been lucky to have only bacillary dysentery, revolting though its symptoms were. The amoebic sort was much more serious and took debilitating years of treatment to bring under control. A biologist on the Hill, who looked for years pale and drawn, had contracted this disease. A good part of every leave he spent in hospital in London undergoing unsavoury treatment that in time, a long time, would get rid of the amoebae, or so it was hoped. The risk of malaria was not taken universally seriously on the Hill. Some people were slack about their tablets; few of us slept under mosquito nets. We chose to rely, rather, on screened windows, the flitgun and waking up to swat cunning survivors. For the fact that most of us were fortunate enough not to catch malaria we should thank not only such precautions as we did take but also, and much more, the efficient British municipal administration.

For the first two decades of this century Kampala had been one of the worst places in the world for malaria. An international conference had been held there so that experts from elsewhere could see for themselves how truly bad things could be and what might be done. A ruthless campaign to drain, remove or clean up every large or minute collection of still water, preferred by mosquitoes for laying their eggs, had not succeeded in eradicating malaria. How could it have, with the African population widely infected and living in an ocean of banana trees whose leaves held water where they joined the stems? Yet these efforts at control had greatly reduced the incidence of malaria in Kampala. Every few days there appeared on the Hill an African inspector armed with a small soup ladle with which he took samples of water. Having peered into storm- and other drains and scattered white powder into them, he would require the removal of any tin can, empty flower pot, toy or anything else that held or might hold even a small amount of water. Anyone who failed to remove a proscribed object could be fined. In fact, most people of all races on the Hill understood the point very well, and co-operated. Then again, the Hill had been cleared, as had Entebbe, as a precaution against not only malaria but also the sleeping sickness that had once been so sinister a risk.

The Uganda epidemic in the early years of this century had killed two-thirds of the lakeside population; it was still a serious danger to man and beast throughout the great areas of East Africa where the tsetse fly ruled. It would spread again wherever man relaxed or withdrew. In spite of all such clearing and other precautions, malaria was everywhere about us. Perhaps in terms of mortality it was, as one authority put it, largely a disease of children, yet survivors went on suffering debilitating attacks. Our staff went down with it from time to time, as did the students. One evening my wife found Nyesi sitting on the grass, still in her green overall, and nearly delirious. She refused to be taken to Mulago: that was where people died, she said. The best my wife could do was give her some aspirin to reduce her temperature and make her more comfortable. Around the Hill, in the urban villages where infant mortality from malaria was still high, the Kampala inspectors, confined by their municipal boundaries, had no authority. Much depended, therefore, on the energy and strictness of the local chief. In fact, conditions in these villages were so insanitary, corrupt and chaotic that in 1954, the year after we arrived, the Kampala Medical Officer of Health drew public attention to what he called "this septic fringe" that constituted "a serious threat to the health of the citizens of Kampala".

Instead of promoting the necessary action, these remarks led to racial tension: the upper class Baganda feared any encroachment on their authority as threatening all the privileges that the established order conferred upon them. There was little or no evidence, they argued, of epidemics spreading from the urban villages into Kampala.

Nevertheless, there were individual casualties. While a friend of ours on the Hill, who was infected with malaria and was in a dangerous condition for some time, probably caught it on one of his frequent safaris, an American researcher who lived on the edge of the Hill, close to one of the villages, caught it there and died. He, we were all sure, was a victim of the gross inadequacy of Buganda municipal government.

Not long before we arrived at Makerere one of the academic staff had died of polio. As newcomers we were told with awe of this dreadful event. What nobody thought to mention was how dangerous it could be simply to get away somewhere nearby for a weekend. After three months of long hours and the demands of adaptation, we needed a break. Where to go, we asked: not too far. Opinion was unanimous that a hotel on the lake near Masaka was the place. Informal, quiet, a beautiful setting, nothing much to do, only 60 or so miles away, it sounded ideal for a restful weekend. So it was, in all respects save one. We enjoyed sleeping under nets in our separate bungalow, with paraffin lamps instead of electric light. The gardens were beautiful, the food reasonably good. Out in Lake Victoria we could see the Sese Islands, until recently deserted because of sleeping sickness but now beginning to be resettled.

We walked down to the beach across an idyllic meadow where Charles, coming up to two, greatly enjoyed tumbling in the grass. We returned refreshed to Makerere. A few days later we noticed a dark spot behind his ear as he played in his bath. A mole, we said: we had not realised he had one there. Then, to our horror, the mole grew to be a disgusting grey tick which we plucked off. Charles soon fell sick. The Hill's voluntary resident physician, David Allbrook, comparatively newly arrived from England, was puzzled: the symptoms could indicate various diseases. His first thought was meningitis.

The days dragged on. We took turns, my wife more than I, in sitting up to keep watch through the nights as Charles became worse. After a week of this, on her return one morning from shopping in Kampala, she held out her arms to him. Unable to walk, he tried to reach her on his knees, one leg dragging. Frantically she called David again to say that each day there was a worse shock. Were we going to lose him? Now polio became the likely diagnosis. David drove off urgently to call in a colleague from Mulago.

He returned with a haggard man, an authority on tropical diseases who had spent years in the Sudan. Our African servants, sympathetically silent and curious, had crowded into Charles's bedroom doorway. Brusquely the newcomer sent them out: "And get that dog out of here!"

After a brief examination he asked if we had been off the Hill. Only to Masaka. Did we not know that Masaka was in a tick-typhus area? We did not. Told of the tick, he had all he needed: having prescribed aureomycin he left abruptly to drive back to his long line of African and Asian patients. Our inadequate expressions of thanks trailed out behind him, followed his ravaged face with its lines deep from a career of determined struggle, new every morning, against the cunning of disease, against the pleasant land that nurtured it, against the society that played host to its exuberant shapes. His visit, of infinite value to us, had lasted ten minutes at most. Needless to say, we obtained the antibiotic immediately. That night my wife had her first good rest since the illness began while a friend, David McMaster, and I sat up with Charles and watched as the drug started to have its miraculous effect.

When we left England Charles had been too young to be inoculated against typhus. Even so, it was our ignorance that had been central to his falling sick. We should have been warned, save that others were no doubt as ignorant. The genial sunshine of paradise (was it now demi-, quasi-, or pseudo-?) lulled the Hill into complacency. Even the prevalence of disgusting jigger fleas failed to convince us all of greater dangers. By burrowing into the foot to lay eggs, the female flea causes a dreadfully itchy bump. To avoid festering, one probes with a needle to evict the flea and draw out her revolting jelly-bag of eggs. Old hands shrugged off this common torment with: "Don't wear sandals, and if you get jiggers, African women are expert at winkling them out for you."

From the time of Charles's typhus, however, we had no illusions about where or how vulnerable we were. Makerere was no doubt a blessed isle, yet around it lay traditional Africa, an immeasurable reservoir of dangers, not only to health: the tsetse fly, always ready to take over, constantly threatened livelihood as well as life. As a new start, we took seriously the menace of diseases conveyed by unseen parasites. Quickly we did our best to learn what to avoid. Take the exceedingly common bilharzia that lurked in still, fresh-water pools or the shallows of lakes and rivers. Under the surface minute water-snails act as hosts to an organism whose immature offspring bore into the human body through any part of the skin. Once inside their unsuspecting victim these invaders turn themselves into little flatworms, both male and female, which wriggle their way up to the liver. There they create havoc by mating. Their eggs then lie low in bowel or bladder until they burst forth to seek a snail and begin again a cycle that has been going on since man's most ancient days. Moral, once you know this entrancing story: obvious. Yet sensible precautions could be no absolute safeguard in other cases.

We kept down flies in the house, naturally, but could not eradicate them. Then there were the garden, the Hill, and Africa beyond, as the case of Richard Livingstone (see biographical index) showed all too dramatically. He came out to stay with us shortly after he retired as president of Corpus Christi College, Oxford. Courteous and wise, if a trifle censoriously whiskery, he had the charming habit of speaking as though he had just come from breakfast with Plato in a peaceful Oxford garden. Two days before he was to fly home we noticed a red bite on his nose. A mosquito has been at him, we thought, or one of the various sorts of fly in the garden. When we saw him off his nose was a little swollen. A day or so after he arrived back in Oxford, Lady Livingstone sent us an agitated telegram. He had returned very ill and had been taken immediately to hospital. There the physicians were puzzled. Had we any idea, she asked, from our knowledge of conditions in Uganda, what might be wrong with him. We set about consulting members of the medical faculty. The telegram had mentioned fever and a greatly swollen and discoloured nose. Little enough to go on, they said; in any case, diagnosis at long range was a fool's game. Someone less conventional thought to mention that recently there had been a small outbreak of anthrax near the market. Worth giving it a try, he said. By this time an even more urgent telegram had arrived: the patient was much worse. We replied with the news of anthrax. So it turned out to be. Fortunately, he recovered.

Buganda's humid climate discouraged exercise but for the most part Europeans on the Hill remained healthy. So much so that Bernard de Bunsen, under heavy pressures daily, used often to say, truth masquerading as humour, how he longed for "a small illness, nothing serious," just enough to keep him out of the office for a few days. Although we were all perhaps not as vigorous as we might have been if somewhere temperate, at least we drank far less alcohol, on the average, than the staggering amounts reputedly consumed by Europeans on out-of-the-way stations. European women at Makerere and similar places did complain that living there had ruined their complexions. One wife was always held up as proof. She had come out, it was said, as a lovely bride, beautifully and vividly English. Now, ten years later, she was faded, sallow, tired. Not all loss of beauty, of course, could be attributed to Africa. One elderly, genial professor cared with loving long-suffering for his kindly, dumpy, plain and complaining wife through her succession of illnesses both real and imagined. Often he would say to us, puzzled that life could have treated him so cruelly: "But you should have seen her when she was younger".

Whether she harboured the same thought about her portly husband we never knew. European women generally developed a sickly-seeming pallor and hair clammy from the humid heat. Their eyebrows flourished. Nor was the appearance of some improved by one effect of East Africa, a heightened hysteria that, since saintliness is necessarily rare, caused embarrassingly ugly explosions of spleen and frustration. One woman in particular, distinguished for her charitableness to Africans and Europeans alike, often strode about the Hill, furiously hot, with ravaged, sidelong glances of suppressed rage. "I've been back just a week," she said once after leave, "and I'm already screaming at everybody!"

Children, too, looked pale as they grew. Charles was regarded as an admirable oddity for keeping his ruddily English looks. Of course, we pointed out, he is active, rarely still.

"My son," replied a friend sadly, "is active too. Even at night he fights other boys in his sleep, yet he grows only paler."

It is possible that the climate affected male beauty too. I had met in England a man who had retired after long service at the old Makerere. He may have been in his late fifties. His slow and crinkled appearance reminded me of my much-loved boyhood pet tortoise, so I was well-disposed towards him, but whether his looks could be blamed on Uganda I could not tell. For conditions that might be thought more serious than the state of one's complexion, Europeans could turn to the small European Hospital in Kampala and be well and comfortably cared for.

For Africans and Asians it was a different story. The teaching hospital, Mulago, was undoubtedly a great centre for the study and treatment of tropical diseases. Our colleagues in the medical faculty felt privileged to practise and teach there. Their patients, too, were clearly fortunate, whatever their fears, for treatment was free. Yet the press of sufferers was great, the crowd of supporting relatives daunting. These relatives were not superfluous: they brought patients the tribal food they were accustomed to. In these arduous conditions it was not surprising that many Africans who had come to Mulago for treatment felt that they had not received sufficient sympathy, whether from European or African doctors. Those who could afford it often preferred to trust in the Church Missionary Society hospital at Mengo which charged fees according to means.

Frequently patients left Mulago far too early in order to seek magical help from an African "doctor" outside and willingly to pay high fees for the privilege. Or they might visit the magician first, especially if they were suffering from what they called an "African disease", because he would make them feel more comfortable than they could be with European medicine. Often, in fact, he would give them such reassurance that they recovered. Typically the "doctor" would hand the patient a basket of leaves containing some herbs and water. "Go home," he would say, "and tonight wash your body with these herbs and water. Then leave the empty basket at a crossroads. After that, sleep, and you will recover."

The theory behind these actions seemed to be that the disease would abandon the patient and transfer itself to passers-by. At other times, recourse to magic meant that the patient arrived at the hospital in desperation and too late. The many diseases treated at Mulago had developed against a general, debilitating background of hookworm (and consequent anaemia), bilharzia, malaria, increasing venereal disease, and widespread malnutrition (kwashiorkor for the weaned babies). Africans' conception of themselves as young or old differed greatly from Europeans'. Men of forty would call themselves old, as would women in their thirties. Given an expectation of life for Africans in East Africa of probably less than forty years, this was not as unreasonable as it may sound. What Africans found impossible to understand or accept was that a young person should die. When that happened, instead of looking for natural causes they might suspect poison, or a racial conspiracy against their tribe, or more likely that someone among their own people had cast a malevolent spell on the deceased. As a student put it to us, such an event produced feelings of deep and hostile grievance: "Europeans never die, Asians die sometimes, but Africans, they are dying all the time."

They were dying, frequently in infancy, or at as young an age as the English did in their towns in the first half of the nineteenth century. By the fifties, however, it was not always the young. In the moonlight, late one evening, I met an African coming away from Mulago, stumbling along under the burden across his shoulders of a long parcel wrapped in the traditional, ochre-stained bark cloth. A Kikuyu student with me asked him in Swahili what it was. The Muganda stopped, greeted us, and replied politely that it was the corpse of his aged father whom he was carrying home for burial. The student, appalled at the thought of what I might feel obliged to do, hurriedly whispered that it would be bad manners to offer to help in such a private matter.

Chapter 7   Firearms, Settlers, Milk and Sex

Visitors to Makerere in the fifties, whether from East Africa or else-where, whether sympathisers or sceptics, always assumed the Hill to house a close community: since the prospect pleased, man too must fit the idyll. Here was a haven, they thought, where all forces united with a will, even evangelically, behind the African interest, whatever that was taken to be. In a broad, vague sense this judgment was true as far as the staff was concerned. A university college devoted to educating Africans was bound to attract to itself men and women of goodwill towards such a project. Yet having said that, it became clear on closer acquaintance with the Hill that goodwill there took many forms. In fact, at any particular time a visitor might have been excused for concluding that the community was split into factions. Longer obser-vation would have revealed that opposing opinions, feeding on concentrated gossip, would form, dissolve, re-group according to the issue of the moment. Membership of one side or the other could not be assumed with full confidence. The Hill had its own politics, its deals and ententes. As an elderly physicist confided to us soon after we arrived, Makerere was hardly "a nest of humming birds". Yet there were one or two divisions broad enough to encourage the discerning to predict how their colleagues would react to whatever came up; even to feel aggrieved if their prediction turned out to be wrong.

The most fundamental of these arose from religion. In the past, Roman Catholics and Protestants in Uganda had slaughtered each other with traditional enthusiasm. Such violence was long over. It was not conflict or suspicion between denominations that was now the question at Makerere. The Roman Catholics stood peacefully apart and did their good in their own way. Through the rest, however, there ran a significant fissure. A powerful minority, lay Evangelicals, had taken a job on the Hill at the intimate behest of their religion. The majority, on the other hand, were there either with no such prominent under-pinning of faith or with a belief of the lukewarm, conventional, Church of England sort that comfortably confined religion within good manners and good deeds. The minority, fervently Evangelical, shared a common, wide-eyed, virtuous look of innocent but knowing and unassailable commitment. They believed themselves to have been called personally to ensure that higher education in East Africa was in their sense Christian, that it did not waste on secular ambition the guided promise of the mission secondary schools that almost all the undergraduates had passed through. Such believers were a true faction, for they had formed a lay staff group that met regularly to pray together and explore the implications of Bible study for policy issues on the Hill. They were acutely concerned with what they took to be Africans' sensi-tivities and feelings. Here, it was clear, was nineteenth century British missionary zeal in a new guise, intent on sustaining the life-giving Word among what everyone assumed would be the new African élite. Only if suitably guided by themselves could education for Africans be the key to an enlightened future.

Among the majority of Protestants and others, not a faction, more a rabble shading off into private unbelief, there were interesting differ-ences. A few congratulated themselves aggressively on their conviction that it actually did Africans a great deal of good, whether they were students or servants, to be roundly abused if they had made some mistake. "Umpumbafu," these models of irascibility would say with res-onant satisfaction, "that's the word, 'stupid clot'". Why not be oneself, why not say straight out what one thinks, they would ask over a drink. That a loud, red-faced barrage of oaths and accusations might be taken sportingly by some Africans but not others seemed not to concern them. After all, Africans had an obligation, hadn't they (glare, bristle), to face up to civilisation and enter it? At this point the newcomer could expect to be regaled with a stripped-down version of Philip Mitchell's account of Africans' backwardness and ignorance towards the end of the nineteenth century, when Europeans arrived in East Africa.

They had no wheeled transport and, apart from the camels and donkeys of the pastoral nomads, no animal transport either... no roads or towns; no tools except small hand hoes, axes, wooden digging sticks and the like; no manufactures and no industrial products except the simplest domestic handiwork; no commerce as we understand it and no currency (save where) barter... was facilitated by the use of small shells; they had never heard of working for wages. They went stark naked or clad in the bark of trees or the skins of animals... had no means of writing... or of numbering except by their fingers or making notches on a stick... no weights and measures of general use... There was a great variety of language... They were pagan spirit or ancestor propitiators, in the grip of magic and witchcraft, their minds cribbed and confined by superstition.

No matter that in 1860, before colonisation, the widely-travelled Richard Burton had found East African peasants' lives, wherever the slave trade was slack, more desirable than those of even the better-off European peasantries. Or that Mitchell's description had encouraged some twentieth century contrarians, idealisers of the primitive such as Elspeth Huxley, to envy those traditional Africans. Let our students learn to catch up like men, so the Makerere tirade would continue, not like the weak-kneed and spuriously special cases befriended by the sectarians. If students could not pass their chemistry test, for example, if they were useless at the subject, best to tell them so in no uncertain terms. No point in praying together. Another beer? Yet we· observed that such "characters" sprinkled between their immoderate outbursts a liberal dressing of unobtrusive decency. No doubt it would strain credulity to mimic their sentimentality by talking of their hearts of gold, but undergraduates on the whole found them funny rather than terrifying. When their students had done good work it was patent how proud of them (and of themselves, of course) these fire-eaters were.

Between such choleric temple-shakers and milder mannered sceptics like ourselves there was a world of difference in occasional behaviour and, above all, of self-image. Our cooler temperament sought self-justification in neither an Evangelical summons nor fierce iconoclasm. We needed no special reasons for trying to do the job we had taken on. It was sufficient to be working (without condescension, we hoped) with and for Africans because one's cosmopolitan goodwill had

93

happened to find itself engaged there at Makerere. It might just as well have been somewhere else. The imperial clock was running down – we knew that – had in fact virtually stopped at home in Britain. There was therefore an enormous amount to be done, and as fast as possible. What we did not realise for the first few years was that it was already too late. Our goodwill was real and on a personal level effective. Yet that could be as nothing against the sinister forces of tyranny and deprivation re-grouping in the dusk, in this land where kulya meant both "to eat" and "to become a chief". Meanwhile the quasi-paradise on Makerere Hill was an entrancing theatre for sustaining all manner of other illusions.

Among the sectarians too, of course, differences of temperament and experience showed up. The great wellspring of the Call became miasmal as it flowed out among the endless and tediously complex sandbanks of this world. For one thing, students were quick to exploit whatever concessions a profession of religion might offer: most students everywhere soon become expert at playing the system. For another, life on the Hill had a way of toning down initial enthusiasms. The climate, possibly? Growing recognition of Makerere's artificial separation from the societies around it? Or perhaps protracted, close familiarity with the few fellow-Evangelicals bred... If not that exactly, then at least impatience, restlessness, a faint quickening of scepticism as so-and-so held forth yet again, eyes alight with assurance.

One of the younger members of this faction, an exceptionally open and candid man (it was he who revealed to me the existence of the prayer and discussion group) told me that he had come out at the behest of a specific Call to Makerere. Now, he confessed, after three years of East Africa he was going home disillusioned, sobered, still a believer but much less simple-minded about Africa than when he had answered the Summons.

Another charming sectarian had had the good fortune to hit upon the usefulness of an extended ecumenism long before others took it up. He avoided the frustrations of dealing only with fellow Christians by appointing himself the unofficial supporter and interpreter of Islam, since although there was a mosque on the Hill it had no resident imam. Having achieved this select eminence (he had had to work for it by studying Islamic custom and humbly bearing the curses of an old Moslem to whom he had offered food with the wrong hand) he showed every appearance of going on serenely year after year. He was an unconventional Evangelical, too, in his choice of a wife. An Englishwoman who would have been an asset on any hockey field, she returned to their house one day to find an African burglar in possession. With no evident thought for his feelings she hurled him to the floor, then sat on him until help came. Soon after we arrived on the Hill it was her promisingly unpredictable husband who summed up for us, standing one typically golden evening in the breeze on the ridge near the eucalyptus clump, three differences in policy and attitude that permanently divided the sectarians from the rest.

The first concerned possession of firearms. No sectarian at Makerere (not necessarily true of other missionaries, as we were to discover) would own a gun of any sort or indeed any weapon. Dogs counted as weapons since Africans were said to be afraid of them, which goes to show how sensible Africans can be, but guns were held to be particularly symbolic of the rule of Africans by force rather than by love. He offered this revelation of the inside view in return for our having mentioned that we had not bought a Luger. How fortunately right we were, he cried, but did we know that Professor X owned a small arsenal of guns, one for shooting elephants, others for birds, and so on, not to mention his service revolver. And wasn't that shameful?! His outrage was not from concern for animals, we realised, but arose from obsessive fear of a remote possibility that X, admittedly a fire-eater but hardly, we were sure, a murderer, would one day shoot a student. Or that every day all students would suffer a compounding moral distortion from contemplating the guns in X's cupboard as signifying the gulf between ordained perfect love and reigning political force. In fact, we discovered, most members of staff did not possess guns, not from Evangelical principle but, as in our own case, from a secure sense of the incongruous and because few hunted.

Second, many at Makerere closely associated guns with settlers but the sectarians also considered the latter anathema in their own right. Time and again they told us what a huge difference it made, to what precisely was never made clear, that Uganda had no settlers. Well, yes, Uganda did have a handful, a few relics whom we imagined to be hard-up and suffering from mildew, but fortunately they were off in the foothills of the Ruwenzori, well out of the way. A wise Protectorate Government had stopped that sort of folly early on. Yet, oddly enough, were there not one or two large and successful plantations owned by Asians? Kenya, however, was necessarily a much more sinful place than

Uganda, so the sectarians thought, because it had made the grave mistake of permitting settlers. Even in the recent past, could you believe it, Kenya had actually encouraged thousands of them, and with special help for ex-servicemen, a school for such settlers! Tanganyika had rather more of them than Uganda but had to be congratulated on having fewer than Kenya. It therefore subsisted, distant and hard to place, somewhere between paradise and hell. Of course it had once been German, a mystifying complication. What about Zanzibar? On Makerere Hill few knew much about that exotic island. Whether or not it had settlers, it was bound to suffer from having had a slave-trading line of Sultans and their Arabs, that at least was clear.

Our philo-Islamic informer's third difference in the prolonged game between the sectarians and the rest had to do, in its various forms, with sex. The faction's view of student sex seemed to be that if left to itself, if a matter of purely African life, it was necessarily a bad thing. Doctors at Mulago Hospital, some of them Evangelicals, had been known to question patients about their marriages. On learning that they were polygamous, the usual situation, these medicos would then indicate that there was no need to look further for causes of the patients' deplorable condition. Our Makerere faction's conclusions were no more generous. Failing denial, if supervised, channeled, conducted according to mission-acceptable constraints and proprieties within a Christian marriage, they conceded that African sex had to be tolerated. Protestant and Catholic missions alike conducted propaganda on behalf of Christian marriage on other grounds too. One, implicit in attitude, was that it was socially superior to customary unions. A great many Africans who accepted this benefit found the constraints of Christian monogamy unbearable. So much so that although it was illegal in Uganda, by Protectorate law, for an African to contract a customary marriage while bound in an undissolved Christian union, nobody was ever prosecuted under this section despite the many opportunities. Another mission doctrine, this one explicit, was the anthropologically shallow teaching that it was immoral to "buy" a wife with bride-price, as was thought to happen in customary marriage, because that reduced the woman to a disposable commodity. Africans, of course, were well aware that this custom of theirs recognised the bride's place within her own clan and family. As they saw it, bride-price tended to keep unions stable, for the goods handed over to the woman's family by the bride-groom would have to be returned if the marriage were to fail.

Much more needed to be said about both settlers and African sex than the sectarians allowed. Who was a settler, exactly? Who qualified for this load of stated and implied obloquy? An Asian born in East Africa, with his own business there and intending to stay until he died, did not. He might control great property holdings, for Asians owned most of the larger hotels in Nairobi and much of Mombasa and Dar-es-Salaam, not to mention extensive plantations, yet he was excluded from being considered a settler by the snobbish English prejudice against trade: he did not count. According to the simple, orthodox answer, a settler was a European who owned land and farmed it, or initially intended to. The implications attached by the faction to that definition were many: for example, that although most settlers believed they had firm title to the land they had cleared and worked, in law rightly so, Africans had a prior moral claim to it, one not recognised by British law but no less vivid or real to Africans because of that. For was it not obvious that Africa must have belonged to the Africans in general? Such a position forgot the long-standing tribal wars that the Europeans had stepped into and stopped, or the fact that so much of the land staked out by settlers had been undeveloped bush. There was also the tacit assumption among the Makerere sectarians that settlers treated Africans with contempt, exploited them, set them a bad example morally by getting up to all sorts of "white mischief" such as drinking, shooting and fornicating. As one irreproachably moral Kenyan white protested to me, "in Uganda you think every settler in Kenya keeps an African bint in a hut at the end of his garden".

Further, the faction thought, settlers could always be relied upon politically to serve their own narrow interest, never that of the indigenous tribes whose welfare and long-term progress towards self-government had been a cornerstone of British official statements, continuing a colonial policy that dated from before East Africa was colonised. Here the Makerere sectarians had a point of sorts. There had undoubtedly been understandable confusion in Kenyan politics between the economic question of the colony's need for European capital and enterprise, and the different but not necessarily separable question of some Europeans' fantasies of permanent political and social domination there.

Yet there was the puzzling case of the respected professor at Makerere, a bachelor neither sectarian nor fire-eater, who had just bought a property in Kenya – "for my retirement", he would say, judiciously recruiting sympathy – and planted it with trees that should mature at just the right time. Nobody believed he would suddenly take to drink, Wild West shooting sprees, or tumbling loose women as soon as he retired; or, for that matter, on his visits to Kenya in the interim. His contemplation of the space at the bottom of his garden would surely remain entirely horticultural. Moreover, there seemed to be something noble and useful about planting trees. Could one dare suggest, then, that some settlers might have what the sectarians would consider a good influence, without which Africans would carry on cutting without proper regard to climate and erosion? Would the faction have to modify its original, absolute condemnation of settlers by considering the sort of farming they went in for? Was forestry benign but mixed farming reprehensible? Alas for this promising distinction, there was the inconvenient case of the milk supply.

When we arrived at Makerere, milk was without doubt a problem. An intriguing choice lay before us. We could use imported, tinned milk, undoubtedly safe but equally certainly nasty, guaranteed to ruin the taste of tea and fur one's teeth. Or we could buy local, fresh milk. Perhaps "fresh" is too optimistic. Possibly "milk" is too. It was hawked around by a battered-looking African who pedalled a contraption like a Walls ice-cream cart. Inside the box was a can from which he ladled alleged milk into one's jug. What sort of animal this liquid had exuded from was never quite clear. If from local cattle it seemed unkind to take milk from such bony, misshapen creatures. The fluid, a dirty white, contained solid pieces, generally dark. Could this have been why, when we first had tea with Bernard de Bunsen, he poured not only the tea through the strainer but the milk too? We judged it prudent to put up with the lesser barbarity, the revolting tinned stuff. Imported tinned cream was also available, particularly used, we noticed, by the sectarians. It should have had a guarantee printed on the label that its superbly tinny aftertaste would transform the flavour of even the most unwelcomely delicious tropical fruit.

Then one fair day there came a revolution in milk supply. Enterprising settlers in Kenya, those hitherto frightful dairy farmers, started frequent, reliable deliveries to Kampala of refrigerated, pasteurised, fresh milk sealed in tetrapaks. Life was transfigured. Untainted afternoon tea, for those who took it with milk, was possible again. In those days before air conditioning, Makerere offices opened at 7.30am and closed each day at 4pm, by which time, in my office at least, the temperature had been well up in the humid eighties since mid-morning. One staggered home over the sunlit grass for tea in the garden, in our case with two mature frangipanis nearby spreading their sweet scent into our deeper shade. Early on we had switched from tinned milk to lemon for afternoon tea; we kept to this habit even after the tetrapak revolution. For the early morning cup, however, it was widely agreed, we were all profoundly indebted to the execrable settlers. With every sip what exquisite pangs of conscience must have stung the more reflective of the Evangelicals!

Had the sectarians, those parochially self-righteous censors, done what we were lucky enough soon to do, got to know some of the settlers, they might have been even more disturbed in their prejudice. One of the college administrators, a kindly man whispered about on the Hill because he was known to swear at people but tolerated because he did so at all races indiscriminately, gave us an introduction to his brother, a settler near Kitale, in Kenya. We called on this monster at his farm, a property with long, airy views that seemed to lift one up as in a glider to the vast spread of skyscape above the slopes of Mount Elgon. We found him a gentle, middle-aged man living peaceably with his wife and their servants in a modest, brick bungalow that might have been lifted out of Sussex. They had not always lived as comfortably. Twenty years before, when they had arrived, there was no house, no farm, just newly-purchased title to land: that is, to bush that had to be cleared. From tents and later from huts they had set to work. No contempt for Africans, no hippopotamus-hide whip on their backs, but wages and a sensible neighbourliness that recognised their different way of life but helped them all the same. They had set up a little school for local children: it had stopped and started again as teachers left and came. Farming had gone no more smoothly. Like most Kenya settlers they had suffered the disasters of adjustment to a strange and harsh continent where every one of a farmer's pigs could be wiped out rapidly by swine fever contracted from warthogs, or all one's cattle infected with rinderpest or other mysterious diseases picked up from the wild.

At times very poor (this was no high "Happy Valley"), for a while they had been unable to afford to buy new shoes for themselves and the children. He had made some himself and soled them with rubber cut from old car tyres. For the children's shoes he had used his wife's worn handbags. Much of their furniture, too, he had made. Small economies persisted in had added up to victory. Vinegar they diluted with equal measures of water, then let it stand to regather strength. By crushing tea on a board with a rolling pin they made it go twice as far. Stale bread and cake they refreshed by brushing it with milk and warming it in the oven. Thus they had persevered, survived, even though often tired out, and now enjoyed a modest success with mixed farming, an example that the local Africans chose not to follow. Here were no rich and aristocratic settlers, no Lord Delamere with his great infusion of capital into the Colony, but in recent years they had had the leisure to develop their garden around the house. Proudly they pointed out that Kenya's uplands allowed them to grow both African and English plants. They gave us tea on their small verandah, then we set off towards Makerere all the readier to be sworn at by their brother. Other settlers whom we came to know in time showed the usual range of outlook and temperament, the variety of social status, that one finds anywhere. Some, of course, as we shall see, were poisonous, others bizarre, but many whom we met were far removed from the stereotype of insensitive, depraved and brutish European, commonly used unthinkingly on the Hill but that lurked in particular behind that extreme attitude of Makerere's sectarians, their horror of the supposedly ungodly settlers.

Compared with the complexities of our informant's third difference between the faction and the assorted others, which he found in their different attitudes to African sex, questions of settlers and politics might be thought simplicity itself. Take, as a start, an academic earthquake that had split the Hill. When we arrived the aftershocks of this local cause célèbre were reverberating strongly, the parties still uncomfortable together. At the dispute's shuddering crisis people had even cut each other on their evening stroll. We were intrigued to find so many – protagonists, antagonists and bystanders – taking us aside to tell us about it. As far as we could make out from all these conflicting and emotional accounts, the story was as follows. A recently-arrived lecturer in fine art had decided that the young African painters and sculptors in the School of Fine Art would not develop as far as they might unless taught in ways accepted in similar schools in Europe and North America. In particular, he believed drawing from live, nude models to be essential. Unfortunately, such had never been part of the art curriculum at Makerere. Nor had it been practised there by the staff in their personal work, this in a part of the world where, in spite of much prudish, mission-induced covering up, acres of innocently revealed skin were readily available for inspection in the countryside. We had at first great difficulty in seeing what all the fuss could have been about. Gradually it transpired that the sectarians, hostile to drawing from the nude, saw in it the certainty of releasing violent African eroticism. Picasso and company were salacious enough – see what anatomical detail they had so pruriently peered into – but if African art students were let loose on live nudes the classes would deteriorate into, well, orgies too easily imaginable. Makerere's reputation would be ruined among the missionaries who ran the only secondary schools. Africans too, "the better sort", would be shocked: upper-class Baganda, in this respect Victorian philistines all, would be outraged by nudity in art. "Just think, what would the annual show of students' work be like!" one formidable Evangelical woman said to us.

This we did, pleasurably, for a minute or two. While the faction found it acceptable for Sam Ntiro to paint his late and etiolated fauvist fantasies of blue, green or yellow cows, or for Gregory Maloba to sculpt in the style of Rodin's Burghers of Calais but more heavily blocked in, they saw nothing wrong with the likes of Njau having to make do with representations of the human figure that seemed ignorant of what could be propping up and filling out the draperies.

The lecturer who, presumably unwittingly, had precipitated this profound cleavage of opinion had felt obliged to resign. Or was he pushed, the fire-eaters had fervently asked, gleefully adding the appeal of academic freedom to their newly-acquired cause of aesthetic tradition. Personality and the animosities of the religious difference itself must have played their part in all this but the specific root of the affair had been sex. What a pity that all those beautiful subtleties of colour in African backs could not be explored and recorded because of prudish constraints on painters. For on this matter the faction had clearly won the day by persuading authority of the political, not the aesthetic, justice of their case. The rest had allowed themselves to be manoeuvred into the untenable position of appearing to argue for indecency, for licensed who-knows-what.

Not all disputes about sex went the same way. There was the issue of dances. The students, as everywhere, wanted to hold them; what is more, now in their halls of residence – with bedrooms available all along the corridors, objected the sectarians! The idea of dances scandalised some of them and disturbed them all. At once they threw up obstacles. Where, for example, were the women to come from? There were only a few women undergraduates compared with the masses of men, far too few to make a dance feasible. Women from the town would bring in venereal disease, the faction pointed out, thus revealing what they thought African dances necessarily led to. The students were ready with an outflanking response. Surely, they argued in their rapid, angular English, the teaching hospital across the valley at Mulago had a large number of African nurses, as did the Church Missionary Society hospital (shrewd blow!) on Mengo Hill.

My own small contribution to their case was to suggest that they offer to police their dances themselves. Their arguments proved unanswerable, their enthusiasm irresistible. So permission was given to hold dances every month, this in spite of the fact that early in 1953 the leading topic of conversation among Africans in Buganda was whether they should be allowed to dance in the European style. Support was strong among the Baganda for their government's attempt to ban such dancing for Africans. That their women should make themselves available to Asian and European men without reciprocal exchange for the benefit of African men, they felt vehemently to be unfair. The Baganda thought their women no longer safe from the sexual appetites of Europeans now that European nationalities not previously seen in Uganda were becoming common there. While it had been a question only of the harmless British, there had been no problem! Makerere, where the dancers would be almost all African and the Europeans safely British, must have been seen as not part of Buganda's grievance, for Mengo made no protest.

Our dances were hot, cheerful, expectantly crowded affairs in the high, cleared dining hall, unobtrusively chaperoned by a couple of members of staff and attended usually by a handful more of the well-disposed younger ones. Several times my wife and I were invited to lead off by fox-trotting sedately about for a turn or two before Dionysos took over. After that, some of the students would ask my wife to dance with them, which she enjoyed doing. A faculty wife reproved her with: "We all know you have to do it, it's part of the job, but you don't need to pretend you enjoy it."

There was no drinking at these dances, at least not visibly, in any case greatly less than at any British or American student dance of the time. The noise was full volume, gigantic and invasive. The most popular records, repeated again and again to smiling, sweating applause, were those with the loudest, most insistent, most blatantly sexual base beat.

They gave rise to a clumsy, swaying, Breughel-like style, not at all the sort of thing for a tea dance in the London season.

Sex was not raising its ugly head, as the faction had feared: it was innocently roaring its elemental insistence. At the first of these dances I caught Nicholas Muriuki, a charming, sophisticated Kikuyu, smiling at me enquiringly. Was I pleased with this outcome, he was silently asking, and no doubt could see from my expression that I was. Basil Bataringaya, a handsome, gentle Catholic student from Western Uganda, was there too, happy as we all were. In a very few years he was to find himself a minister in the first government of independence and, though it would have been unimaginable at that first dance, a partner in the Obote regime's oppression. Later he would be pursued into Kigezi by Amin's army thugs when they took over, dragged out from sanctuary in a convent, then roughly decapitated and dismembered, the pieces of him distributed about the district, his head displayed with the terrorising question, "Do you recognise this man?" Also present that night of the first dance was Mwai Kibaki, a serious, self-contained young man of evident ability, soon to rise to office in independent Kenya. All these students, men and women, had been working hard and many faced great responsibilities; they deserved their evening off.

Yet one or two of the more squeamish (or sycophantic?) Kikuyu students complained about the dances to Carey Francis, their old headmaster. When he next came to Makerere, for a meeting of the College Council, he raised the matter with me. Such was the flow of modernity into student life, so great the respectability ensured by the students themselves, that in the end he found himself with no case to make. Education, after all, broadens horizons, or so we are assured: it certainly multiplies desires and the arguments to support them. "Have we not been well brought up in our mission schools, then?" the students asked. "Are we not to be trusted?" So Francis backed off with a good grace from championing the faction's cause. This was something of a turning point, for missionaries of all stripes had always condemned African dancing of no matter what sort.

That African students might be as passionate as some Europeans were said to be the Makerere sectarians found frightening. Among their devotees, therefore, they carried out a type of sex-education, rather prurient it seemed to us, clearly aimed at reducing passion. As one of them, a middle-aged spinster, proudly told us, it consisted of a catechism like this. Do you long to do that and that to your girlfriend?

Embarrassed answer after much mumbled hesitation, yes. Then pause, consider, resist. Even where this formula was intended as an aid to women's protection or satisfaction, matters that certainly needed attention, it was coloured by the underlying prejudice against African sexuality. How regrettable, the sectarians used to say, that there have to be school and university holidays, when students go home. We all know what they get up to there, beyond our reach: you can see it on their faces when they return. There is no doubt that in the urban villages and on the Buganda shamba, forms of sexual life went on that were barbarously loose by mission standards.

To what extent such practices differed from what could have been found in Europe or North America is a different question. Looked at from another point of view, some Buganda customs were certainly archaic and morally lax when judged by the standards of certain African peoples further south. We knew in Kampala a sophisticated and charming African woman from South Africa, Noni Jabavu Crosfield, who had been educated in England and was married to a European. She had come to Uganda to see her sister, whose marriage to a Muganda lawyer was failing. As a result, Noni set in progress traditional consultations between the two families, in the hope of reconciliation. Not only did the two sisters find Luganda an archaic language (as English-speakers today might have trouble with Anglo-Saxon) and Buganda morals, heavy drinking, and poor hygiene repugnant, but, as Noni told us, when they were discussing in the family group the wife's sexual preparedness for marriage, they were both nonplussed by the question, "Has she been pulled?"

Noni had an attractive contralto speaking voice: in her puzzlement she almost sang "pulled". Anyone not in the Buganda swim, it seemed to us, might be excused for being similarly at a loss. We could only commiserate, keep our theories to ourselves, and hope that all would work out for the best. What particularly shocked Noni was the Buganda husbands' habit of bedding their wives' sisters, among others. This, by her own Xhosa people's standards, was incest and definitely prohibited.

Faced with complexities like this and numerous other clashes of standards, attempts by the faction to channel and control students' sex life was a losing game. Moreover, what of the sectarians' own sexual and moral health? Who was to catechise these self-appointed guardians? I was surprised one day on my travels, when hundreds of miles from Makerere, to be asked out of the blue by a high official what I thought of a certain model of Evangelical propriety on the Hill. When I asked what the question meant, I was asked in return what I thought of his collection of photographs of African breasts. Had I not been shown them? Didn't I think there was something fishy about that sort of thing? Above all, the faction's views seemed to presuppose, ridiculously, that Makerere could be more than a temporary withdrawal of those few Africans from the tribal or semi-urbanised life around them. Desires and inhibition in the complex depths of African students' experience, things apart from colonial guardians and revealed to them only in glimpses, would still flourish undiminished after missionaries and governors had departed. The view of the "irreligious" rabble at Makerere must surely prevail, that in this matter things would and should take their own course as African students, pressed between several worlds, sought their own ways.

Chapter 8   Uncommon Tasks

꧁꧂

Getting About in East Africa

We missed by half a century the heroic age when Europeans whose destination was Uganda had walked up from the Coast by slow, caravan stages. This had been a hazardous feat in not quite the way it sounds, for wild animals, anxious to get out of man's way, would normally attack only if startled or wounded. Instead, it was the combination of theft, diseases and the Masai that made it so dangerous. Once safely in Uganda, moving about the country in those earlier days had also been slow, gratifyingly so as seen by old hands looking back nostalgically. One, A.R. Morgan, who arrived in Uganda in 1908 as the first cotton inspector, has recorded the gradual changes in transportation before he retired from Uganda service in 1930. At first he went on safari on foot, supported by a team of porters, then progressed through donkey to bicycle, then motorcycle and, eventually, motor car. Of the modes of travel within East Africa available to us latecomers the railway between Kampala and Mombasa via Nairobi was by far the most pleasant. Although well established and reliable, it was unfortunately also the slowest ("unfortunately" because by then we were all infected with modern haste). Journeys by train in Tanganyika, with older rolling stock, were hot and equally slow (two days and nights to Mwanza, on the southern shore of Lake Victoria, from Dar-es-Salaam via Tabora) while offering the privilege of being dusty too, as grit poured in through the unglazed windows. At least for the two days and nights that it took to trundle from Kampala to Mombasa there were clean and

106

comfortable sleeping cabins, if one paid for them, and a good restaurant car. The main attraction of the journey was to be following an historic, pioneering route; the line from Mombasa on the Indian Ocean to Kisumu on Lake Victoria had opened in 1902, the Kampala extension (branching off at Nakuru and by-passing Kisumu) in 1931, each an outstanding feat of engineering. The train would pull slowly out of Kampala, seemingly at little more than a walking pace, and in due course cross the source of the Nile before doubling back to stop at Jinja. Then out and north before it made east for Tororo, soon across the border into Kenya, around the southern base of Mount Elgon and steadily up to Eldoret at 6,800 feet. Up still further it climbed, to the western escarpment of the Eastern Rift Valley, then down at Eldama Ravine to the floor (the gradient here less steep than from Mau Summit to the south, on the older Kisumu line), south-east via Equator to join the Kisumu line just before Nakuru, through Naivasha with its freshwater lake, and up the eastern wall on the other side of the Rift to Escarpment and Uplands, only to descend once more south-east towards Nairobi.

One had the leisure during this majestic progress to think of those who had made the journey from the coast up-country to Uganda before the Great War and until 1931. They had had to leave the train at Kisumu railhead and board the steamer to take them across Lake Victoria to Port Bell for Kampala. The whole journey would have been a pleasantly leisurely introduction to the country, and some of the people one was going to work with. The traveller in the fifties could see all around, too, evidences of how much the railway had done by his day to reduce Africans' isolation in the interior, never absolute previously but always severe. Also to develop the region for farming and commerce as rail transport took over from traditional porterage on the head and the later European or South African bullock carts. The journey contributed, too, unforgettable moments of mystery. To awake in the cold, equatorial night at a halt well up in the Kenya Highlands, as though in some imaginary place, to look out and see Africans in old felt hats and army surplus greatcoats, or wrapped in blankets, to hear them speak an unfamiliar tribal language, their breath visible, not to know where one was, to climb down from the bunk and go to look out of the coach door to find nobody now in sight, only voices in the gathering white of a mist. All this gave one the feeling of strangeness that travellers seek, the disturbing satisfaction of being utterly removed from everyday.

In the daytime passengers had an incomparable chance to grasp the size and scope of the country, the expansive grandeur of its skies with the whole landscape under constant surveillance by patient, high-circling vultures. Beyond Nairobi, as the train descended 6,000 feet in the 300 miles to the Indian Ocean, after the game park (where one saw very few animals in the brief dusk) the views became less interesting, the landscape barren, and the pace seemed even slower. Soon it was bedtime again and one looked forward to waking up in the Coast Province.

Few airfields were capable of taking commercial flights: the pattern of demand, too, limited air travel to journeys between the main centres. For these, of course, it was the quickest way. The twin-engined Dakotas of the East African Airways Corporation, aircraft elderly enough to add a touch of adventure to routine flights, flew at about 8,000 feet, no higher because of the lack of oxygen, so offered views of the country surpassed only by those from a private light aeroplane. On one occasion, as we flew in and out of the clouds on the scheduled run between Nairobi and Entebbe, without warning, the aircraft's door fell off. What excitement in the rushing, buffeting noise, better than driving fast in an open Aston Martin. Aside from such bonuses, air travel was expensive, so much so that we preferred to go by car, as I did whenever there was time when travelling on my job. The places I needed to get to were frequently not served by air, or if they were, I needed the car once I got there. A journey where air travel was particularly useful was the short hop, 45 miles, from Dar-es-Salaam to Zanzibar. Officials in Dar strongly advised me not to hang about waiting for the Zanzibar Government's slow steamer. This flight also had the advantage of offering the sight of exceptionally beautiful shades of colour, vivid bars divided by subtle gradations, in the shallows around this historic island on the continental shelf. At about the time of my visit I marked in our copy of *Freya of the Seven Isles* Conrad's reference to the deep blues and vivid greens of such waters over submerged reefs.

To other, less conventionally exotic places, then, we went by car. That could be hazardous. Garages capable of making repairs were all too literally few and far between, as were petrol supplies. Nobody experienced would set out on a long safari (the term by now used for any longish journey) without a full tank and reserve can (a debe), radiator and oil checked, emergency bottle of water, tool kit, spare fan belt, spark plugs and inner tubes, tyre levers, jack and footpump. Some sandwiches, chocolate and drinking water, too, were a wise precaution. Away from the towns there was little motor traffic: off the few arterial roads, hardly any. There the common hazards were chickens, occasionally a hump-backed cow, heavily loaded and wobbling bicycles, and women walking with burdens balanced on their heads, burdens (or even single bottles) that they expertly kept in place as they leapt out of the way, startled but giggling. The principal danger, however, was the corrugated, alarmingly holed, ditch-lined road itself. No wonder that many motorists had a Nakuru blanket with them in case they were stuck for the night. We always took with us as talisman an old familiar, the heavy blue travelling rug that my wife had had to guard against the chill damp of wartime Oxford.

Before the Second World War the British administration had paid little attention to roadbuilding. As a result, one had a choice: dust in the dry season or mud when it rained. In either case the corrugated road surface tested one's car and, even more, one's nerves. From Kampala to Nairobi, for example, the narrow tarmac lasted to Jinja, then one suddenly found oneself jolting along on murram, a hard red gravel surface, then in Kenya on something inferior even to that all the way until at last, for the stretch from Nakuru and down from the Rift Valley wall to Nairobi, there was the narrow metalled road again, this one expertly built by Italian prisoners of war. At this point, if having driven without an overnight break, one suffered the ghastly, jerking tendency to fall asleep at the wheel. Despite determined grading by the road crews, every surface not metalled was more or less corrugated. In the dry season one had to get up to a certain speed to reduce the juddering to a minimum, but it was always exhaustingly present. Wheels frequently went out of alignment, tyres wore unevenly and alarmingly fast.

Driving at a tolerable speed on dry corrugations carried with it the constant danger of skidding on the loose surface. Our Makerere sculptor, Gregory Maloba, well known for driving fast, even had the misfortune to turn his Volkswagen Beetle over and injure his head seriously. A great cloud of dust accompanied every car. By the end of a long journey one was red with it, hair stiff and clothes stained with a mixture of dust and sweat. To pass a vehicle coming in the opposite direction one hurriedly closed windows and air vents (no air conditioning in those days).

Another hazard was the unpredictable hole in the road. Small ones were plentiful: one simply bumped and crunched through. Deeper ones might qualify for the universally accepted East African warning sign, a branch standing up in the hole. A portable "Genda mpola" ("Go Slow!") out in the country in Uganda meant that either a crew was working ahead or extraordinary caution was called for.

Even more difficult, however, was the rainy season. As compensation for not being dusty, wet corrugations had a relentless tendency to pull the car sideways into the ditch, as happened once to us, with painful injury to my wife's face and teeth. It was vital to keep the speed well down and avoid rapid acceleration. Worse still were the patches of deep mud through which one tried to pick one's way in the generally fruitless hope of not getting stuck. Worst of all were the usually long stretches where the road was being repaired or re-made. There the mud could be so deep and extensive, the scene so chaotic, that if one were inexperienced enough to try to drive through it one would have only the hope that a roadworker would appear on his bulldozer and tow one out. In this way the road crews were most helpful: it was merely a matter of waiting until one of them turned up, as we had to do for two or three hours near Kapenguria once, when Jomo Kenyatta was on trial there. There was little chance that Africans, if any were nearby, would assemble in sufficient numbers to help effectively. Already at that date they were disenchanted with such fortuitous labour on behalf of idiots who would insist on trying to move about in the rainy season when, as every African knew, the accepted and sensible thing was to stay as much as possible indoors, preferably in bed.

Once when I was returning to Kampala from Nairobi I had with me as passenger a visitor of the Principal's from England, a man of about fifty who had flown to Nairobi to see friends. When we had first met him, in Bernard's garden, he had been expansive in the sunshine, hands crossed complacently over protruding belly, quietly joyful as though awakened, astonishingly, in paradise. When I picked him up in Nairobi he had been genial enough but soon, out on the road, he became exceedingly anxious about the long journey. After we left the metalled section we had the bad luck to run into the worst road conditions that I had experienced, many miles of excessively poor, muddy surface, the consequence of unexpectedly extended rains. Twice we were stuck and waited to be towed out. Ahead, a road worker cheerfully shouted from his bulldozer cab, things were worse.

My passenger fretted and moistly fidgeted. I advised him to relax, pointed out how reliable and sturdy the Peugeot was, that in the East African safari race it had beaten the field. Not like the first car that we had bought out there, I thought to add, one of the early, British-made Ford Consuls. It had proved unsuitable, even dangerous. Its wheels would not stay aligned. It had bounced and slithered on the corrugations. What a good thing we were not driving that! Oddly enough, this helpful information seemed not to encourage him at all. Nor did he smile when I mentioned that on side roads vehicles had often to be abandoned in mud holes for a week or more. Then it occurred to me to disclose that I had obviously been born lucky. Not to worry. Had I not in the war survived a forced landing without power into irregular little fields with stone hedges and, rushing up under the starboard wing as we side-slipped, spiky, anti-glider ground obstacles along the beach nearby? Was it not significant, too, that later I had walked away from two crashes? Strangely, even this persuasive argument failed to convince him. He merely sweated and groaned all the more, looked drawn and greyer, entertained me at length with tales about his past encounter with kidney stones (which he attributed to his having gorged himself all one summer on tomatoes), and leaned exaggeratedly against the car when-ever we navigated around a pit.

During the afternoon, after already eight wearying hours on the road, we found ourselves within reach of a railway halt. At least, that is what the Shell road map seemed to suggest. When I mentioned where I thought we were, it was as though with a great, feathery rush an archangel had hovered down to him with tidings of rescue. I told him that there were no airfields nearby but that the trains were safe in all weather. Perhaps he might like to catch the next one? There was no place in the world he wanted more to be at that moment than on a platform with the train steaming in on time.

After various incidental troubles we did manage to slither our way to the halt. My passenger's spirits revived with visions of fast trains to London from the tidy dormitories of Sussex. The Assistant Stationmaster, a dignified and courteous Asian, explained that, yes, there was a train to Kampala with a restaurant car and possibly a sleeper, but not, unfortunately, for another 24 hours. The nearest hotel? Yes, sir, only about 30 miles down the road, an establishment run in fact by his brother-in-law. No doubt there was a less well-provisioned train? Nothing for passengers at all today, only a goods train expected in about three hours, a very slow one, of course. Abjectly my companion asked if he could, please, be allowed to travel on that. I reminded him that the Peugeot's seats rolled down to make two beds. Would he not be more comfortable spending the night on one of them? He seemed hardly to hear. The only object left in his blank world was a train, for as Conrad had put it somewhat sententiously, he was one of those whose existence is made possible only among civilised, organised crowds, within the confidence that familiar institutions will shelter them from dangerous unknowns, from the primitive savageries of man and nature. Thus it was that shortly after dark I found myself hoisting this much-deflated traveller and his case up on to the bare boards of an empty freight car and receiving haggard and mournful thanks for his share of our sandwiches.

The following afternoon he arrived, safe but hollow, dirty and unshaven, at Kampala station, where I had the pleasure of helping him down again. I had decided to spend the night at the halt and had slept comfortably in the Peugeot. Next morning it was sunny, the road dried out, and I was able to make good time back to Makerere. When I went to meet him I had bathed and changed. On the Hill the poor man was thought less well of for having abandoned me, in East African judgment not a comradely thing to do, for there was always the chance of real dangers such as collision or a mudslide. When Bernard de Bunsen heard of it he frowned, his sign of intense disapproval. For my part, by the time I reached home I was sorry to think of my ex-passenger bumping along so ignominiously in a goods train, but out on the appalling road I had been glad to be rid of his urgent, dramatic and distracting co-driving as he discovered again and again, when he slithered forward almost off his seat, with his right foot thrust agonisingly forward, that the brakes on the passenger side had been disconnected by some malevolent demon. When he got home to England, however, he re-established his equanimity by writing to the East African Railways to thank and praise the Assistant Stationmaster and the caboose crew on the train for their extraordinary succour. The Chief Operating Superintendent of EAR replied with courteous ambiguity that he was having "a suitable endorsement made on their reports".

Side roads could be so greasily slippery, so muddily rutted, as to be impassable literally for weeks. Whether on these or on main roads there was no point in feeling hurried. Even on the best of days one encountered the unavoidable hazard of butterflies and other insects plentifully dashed, and very stickily splattered, against the windscreen and, more seriously, into the radiator grille, where they could cause the engine to overheat. In normally bad conditions the sensible alternative to getting stuck was not to venture into a deep mud patch at all. One soon learned to judge the state of the road ahead. If caught in a downpour or if one came across deep mud recently rained on, one stopped the car and waited. A main road would soon dry out enough in the sun, that is in a few hours at most. On one such occasion in Kenya, miles from anywhere I knew, I got out of the car to stretch my legs and relieve myself. This achieved, I happened to look up at a bank beside the road and was startled to see, close by in the profound silence, an African. He was standing on one leg and leaning on his spear, his other leg bent and resting foot on knee. Almost naked, spare and well muscled, he looked the wildest man I had ever seen, with his hair done up at the back in a large mud bun and his eyes, gazing through and down past me, seeming to say haughtily that I was an intruder and unwelcome. I took him to be a herder, but of what tribe I did not know. Having ventured a hesitant "Jambo," which he ignored, I went back to my solitude in the car, leaving him in his. Like one of Seurat's remote, iconic figures, he remained standing there motionless, wonderfully camouflaged.

Mau-Mau Kenya

Compared with the newness and strangeness of forays into the other East African territories, journeys in Uganda (a little less than the size of Britain or about one and a third times the area of Oklahoma) seemed tamer. Those to the hotter parts north and north-east of Buganda did have the interest of regions where the economy was based on millet, a welcome change from bananas. A previous generation of Agricultural Officers had tried to introduce European methods of ploughing into the cultivation of this nutritious grain, but had succeeded only in causing erosion of the fragile soil. By the fifties a humbler and more effective attitude of learning from and improving upon traditional, far less intensive African practices was starting to prevail. Instead of planting in furrows, Africans would heap up little mounds of soil for their plants, expecting less return of grain for their efforts but at least safeguarding the soil until that plot needed a rest and was left for a long period of fallow. A family journey into south-western Uganda, of which more later, was exceptionally interesting for other reasons but Kenya, Tanganyika and Zanzibar proved even more fascinating when my duties took me that far from the Hill.

When we first arrived at Makerere the Mau-Mau rebellion among the Kikuyu was in full swing. This, naturally, had consequences on the Hill and, to various degrees, throughout East Africa. Kikuyu students at the college, under increasing strain, knew very well what was happening at home, where their people lived under the enormous pressure of tribal solidarity for everyone to take the first Mau-Mau oath. By this they swore never to divulge the movement's secrets and, for example, to steal arms and money; also to behave in various more trivial ways judged by the movement to be anti-European, such as drinking African beer rather than European bottled. Some students told us that almost everyone in the tribe had taken this first oath, for "oathing" to maintain cohesion had long been part of Kikuyu custom. Those who held out against Mau-Mau were commonly murdered, women and children not spared, when the terrorist gangs came down from the high forests on the Aberdares. Many fewer, we were told, had taken the much more serious second oath. By this the juror committed himself, under pain of the dreaded curse of the oath-breaker, to kill a European when called upon to do so. Fewer still had been subjected to the third. This used sexual practices taboo in Kikuyu society, and even cannibalism, to make the wretched oath-taker feel such an outcast that he would be willing to do anything on the way to his death, the only release from his pollution.

Many of the Makerere Kikuyu had managed to avoid involvement in any of this. Away at their mission boarding schools they had been safe from tribal pressure. If they had been able to get to Makerere without going home they remained secure. Several kept up this isolation by staying at the college during the vacations. Those who went back almost certainly had to conform to the first degree. One at least, to our knowledge, Kinyanjui, a Christian from the Alliance High School, had gone back, had publicly refused to take the oaths, and had been in great danger as a result of his prominent courage. However removed our students managed to remain, in body and mind, from participation in the rebellion, they knew that for their families there could be no such escape. The police and military, they were convinced, were harassing their people just as much as Mau-Mau threatened them from the forests. If students wished to go home for the vacation they had to seek special passes and were subject to interrogation. Even at Makerere many Kikuyu felt they were being watched.

It all amounted to a first class recipe for tensions and unhappiness. We thought it a tribute to the students' good sense, and probably largely thanks to their youth, that so many of them remained cheerful and friendly. Their friendships among themselves must have been a great solace: one saw couples of the young men strolling hand in hand, showing not to the world but for themselves a poignantly simple solidarity. Relations between staff and students continued generally relaxed and cordial. Humour was appreciated and always helped. One evening in hall I had the job of saying goodbye on everyone's behalf to a chemistry lecturer who was going back to England. I reported that recently he had observed me tearing off a number of the perforated page corners in my Oxford University diary. For some time I had forgotten to do it.

"Aha," he had said, "I see. On this system you find out the date by weighing the diary."

Immediately there was a huge burst of laughter at his quintessentially chemistry witticism, and it was laughter that went on. At that moment one might have thought Mau-Mau and all the other troubles the remote concerns of another planet. Some of the undergraduates, however, as we well knew, did suffer abysmally. There were those who became depressed and sought our help with problems at home or, a common difficulty, with genuinely acute shortage of money. Others, a few, broke down in various ways under the strain of the contrast between home and Makerere or because of conflicts within themselves.

"Do not think," one student warned us with deep feeling, "that Europeans elsewhere in East Africa behave towards us as you do here on the Hill."

He may have had in mind, for example, our practice, deliberately adopted as soon as we arrived, of addressing students as Mr or Miss So-and-So. They clearly appreciated this formality as a courtesy and found it useful as a shelter. It became one small thing among countless others that went towards the special atmosphere of Makerere.

One man whom I knew, but not well, refused to come out of his room. Friends' enquiries through the door produced the answer that he was sick. Against the rules they charitably put down food for him: sometimes he took it in but nobody saw him do it. Our doctor called to him through the door but he gave no reply. I thought I might try. When I knocked, no sound. I called his name. Eventually there was a rustling inside, the first sign of life I had heard. Then the door was unlocked and left open an inch. He was scurrying back to bed. After waiting a few seconds I went in. To my horror the reason for his seclusion was all too obvious. He lay on his iron bedstead in dingy sheets, his face and upper body covered in pustules that gave off a disgusting stench. All his skin, he whispered, was similarly affected.

He agreed to have the doctor visit him but insisted that he would not leave his room to go into Mulago hospital. The doctor, naturally, wanted him in the sick bay as soon as possible but failed to persuade him. Next morning, when I called to see him again, his room was empty. He had simply walked away, nobody knew where. He must have been forced into taking the second oath and was suffering under the curse, said another Kikuyu student whom I knew well enough to discuss such things with. Or he may have believed himself bewitched.

We never saw him again but my friend's theory was supported some weeks later when a Special Branch officer came to the college to enquire about him. He told us that information of the student's serious involvement had come from Kenya. Another Kikuyu student walked off from Makerere in the middle of term, probably in similar trouble, "to catch the train home" as he told a friend. The alarming thing in his case was that the domestic bursar found his bed soaked with blood, presumably his, and there was a puddle of it on the floor. She called the doctor, who set off quixotically to drive at top speed in his powerful, racing-green car to Jinja, where he hoped to board the train and help the student off it. Anyone hemorrhaging that badly from, presumably, an ulcer, he reasoned, had no business making a long journey. But the student was not on the train. In this case we never heard from or of him again.

At that time there were only about 300 European police in Kenya. It was remarkable that they had managed nevertheless to uncover the Mau-Mau conspiracy before it had achieved its original plan of a much wider uprising. Uganda and Tanganyika had even fewer European police officers. In all three territories the police were forced to rely on the goodwill of voluntary informers. When my wife found herself by chance in the same Luganda class as the head of the Special Branch in Uganda, she was surprised when he said to her, "Now that we have met, perhaps from time to time you could let me know of anything that seems important".

At Makerere it was policy that we should never provide information informally and personally about students or colleagues. If, however, the college were presented with a formal and specific request, it would respond. Nevertheless I was convinced that one or two members of staff regularly gave information to the police. I had no reason to believe that such intelligence was necessarily malicious, or biased against students, or prejudicial to either the staff's or students' freedom of action. On the contrary, I suspected that in general this reporting was benign and supportive of the college's work. Yet the potential for something more divisive and illiberal was undoubtedly there.

It was against this background that I made my first visit to Kenya, a colony the size of the states of New Mexico and Colorado together. First stop, the renowned Alliance High School. On the crest of a ridge up at Kikuyu, it had been founded in the twenties as a boarding school for Anglican and Presbyterian Africans, but was by now open to boys of all denominations. My main purpose was to call on its widely respected and deeply religious headmaster, Carey Francis. In the past he had been publicly critical of what he saw as Makerere's lack of moral guidance of its students. Now, as a Kenya Government appointee on the College Council, he was in an even more powerful position to harm the college's reputation, or so many at Makerere feared, including the Principal and Paul Vowles, the Registrar. Francis was indeed a formidable man, bluff, solid-looking and outspoken, a man secure in his principles and a wholehearted supporter of what he saw as his boys' best interests. In East Africa, schools, missions, district officers and so on often worked with a feeling of isolation, and in most cases the reality of it. They greatly appreciated visits from people whom they would other-wise have known only through correspondence. Bernard de Bunsen therefore thought that if I called on Carey Francis in his lair I should stand a better than average chance of convincing him that Makerere was not playing the Socrates with his young men.

Francis asked me all the expected anti-corruption questions (after all, he cared: he had given up the probability of an outstanding mathe-matical career to devote himself to African education) but proved a more reasonable ogre than I had been led to expect. Roaring, strangely enough, seems often to become louder with distance. We got on sur-prisingly well despite our difference in age and experience (he seemed to be in his fifties). Having cleared something of a path through the thicket of moral influence, we moved on as soon as we decently could to the far more pressing matter of the anti-Christian, anti-Western Mau-Mau movement. His boys, he was convinced, were substantially free of that taint but he feared for them. If the rebellion went on much longer, many would be unable to resist pressures to join whenever they returned home. I asked whether they were safe there at school. Might such a well-known, leading institution in Christian education be attacked, since African Christians and the mission schools had been the Mau-Mau terrorists' principal victims? Was his school not the most important counterweight to the Kikuyu Independent Schools that Jomo Kenyatta had taken over on his return to Kenya? An attack was entirely possible, he thought, but they were prepared. He relied on the boys. All the bigger ones slept with a "panga" under the bed. The panga is a short, heavy, broad-bladed, double-edged tool for cutting cane, bush, etc. It is about the length and, I imagine, the weight of the Roman short sword. This, the commonest Mau-Mau weapon, was typically used in the first assault to hack off hands. His boys, said Francis, would leap into action as soon as they heard the alarm bell. Much as I admired this spirit of standing up for oneself, the venerable headmaster's news gave me much to think about. This possible Christian soldier might not fully have grasped the military implications of his plan.

When it came to bedtime and I retired to the small guest room to write my notes, there was even more cause for doubt. The room had rows of windows on two sides. Each was covered with expanded metal, true, but shooting through that would have been no trouble. The Mau-Mau had proved themselves most ingenious at building home-made guns and adept at smuggling weapons in from Ethiopia. Whichever way I looked at it, my bed was an easy target. There were no curtains or blinds; outside, no lights. So, I thought as I undressed, were there to be an attack, Francis and I could be finished off fast, a rather amateurish way to die. In any case, the prospect of a large number of hefty young Africans, no matter how courageous and well-intentioned, rushing around in the dark waving pangas left me feeling distinctly more endangered than protected. It would have been like Hegel's celebrated night, in which all cows are black. With these fortifying reflections I almost regretted not buying a Luger, climbed reluctantly into the bed so exposed to crossfire and slept soundly until Carey Francis, reassuringly English and pacific in his woollen dressing gown, brought me in a cup of tea at six next morning.

On then to Nairobi for appointments with various officials, but first to meet the representative of the International Confederation of Free Trade Unions, a former Yorkshire steelworker. He had offered to take me to see Tom Mboya, a Jaluo in his twenties who was General Secretary of the Kenya Federation of Labour and already rising in Kenya politics (even so, to have suggested then that he was to be assassinated in 1969 while a member of an independent Kenya's government would have seemed a fantasy extraordinary even for Nairobi).

I was staying at the old-fashioned, sedate Norfolk Hotel (quiet then but having seen fast and riotous earlier days) but had to go over to the brasher New Stanley to meet the man from ICFTU. It was a shock to find the lobby there, which seemed also to be a bar, crowded with young European civilians ostentatiously carrying guns of various sizes. That disciplined men in uniform, soldiers or police, should keep their weapons ready during the emergency did not trouble me. They had their job to do, their orders and codes of conduct to obey. That two elderly settler ladies out on their farm, dining alone by lamplight with their pistols beside them on the table, should have had the presence of mind to notice that their houseboys were nervous and had left the dining room door ajar, should then have had the cool courage to shoot the leading Mau-Mau intruders as they burst in with their pangas, and should have driven off the rest: such preparedness and spirit seemed to me, as to all Europeans, a wonderful example. But that immature civilians should swagger about armed in Nairobi I found disturbing, not only because of the provocation that such behaviour must gratuitously offer but also because rifles and pistols clattering alongside the breakfast beer on lobby tables brought out the worst in flushed faces, an excessive and ugly bravado. That is how it must have been in August 1914 when troops of rashly belligerent settlers rushed to gather in Nairobi and call on their pacific governor to wage immediate war on German East Africa, which lay within sight to the south.

The display in the New Stanley lobby was in sobering contrast to the restrained opinions and demeanour of the European officials with whom I had appointments. Yet I was distressed into speechlessness by one couple whom I came across. Were they lying, fantasising, or telling the appalling truth? At the time I was too horrified to judge. This man claimed that he and two or three other Europeans, cronies of his, would drive out in the middle of the night to find some isolated African houses. They had put on tennis shoes in order to creep about silently and had blackened their faces. They would spray petrol on the houses and set them on fire. Then as the families rushed out they would shoot them down. All this he said lightly as though telling an amusing story at his club. His voluptuous wife, not to be outdone, whispered that she always kept a small revolver tucked in her garter. I could hardly verify that any more than I could her husband's odious boast. Afterwards I concluded that they must have been fantasists but sickening even as such. They seemed too glib for villains, too featherweight their verbal swagger.

As I was to learn, Nairobi's peculiar flavour, part sobriety, part hysteria, sprang from its many contrasts and tensions: between Government and settlers, for example; between missionaries and the wilder settlers; between struggling European expatriate civil servants, crushed by Nairobi's high prices, and the separate rich sets of commercial Indians or aristocratic Europeans; between all of these, along their elegant avenues of blue-flowering jacarandas in the city centre, and the overcrowded African slums poised sullenly around the outskirts.

Tom Mboya received us in his modest office, what Americans call a walk-up. He was of middle height, round-faced, dressed neatly in a khaki suit. His courteous manner, verging on friendly, was nevertheless impressively reserved. Clearly such a man was not about to rush into personal confidences or eager disclosures of policy. As far as it went, what he said about the situation in Kenya was reasonable enough. As a Jaluo he was not tribally involved in the Mau-Mau rebellion: he could see both sides but was unwilling to commit himself on how it would all end. Although naturally a supporter of African education he was suspicious of the new Makerere men about to enter the professions and Government service. His main interest, he let us know, was in building his African trade unions. In that task, he judged, Makerere graduates were unlikely to help. As we talked his character seemed to harden while his manner became more ambiguous. When we parted he remained as unruffled and in some way remote as when we had begun. I was left puzzled, mostly by what had not been said: no openness of conversation here.

Then I realised that he must be used to being watched and reported on by Special Branch. A little later during this visit an official asked me how I had got on with Mboya: it had rapidly gone around the small Nairobi gossip-circuit that I had called on him. I replied that he had seemed a reasonable man, of moderate opinion. That, said the official, was the impression he had wanted to give: he was expert at telling others what they wished to hear. His English-speaking persona was quite different from his Swahili-speaking, in which he would break into devastating imitations of Europeans speaking bad Swahili, a performance that left Africans falling about with laughter. Europeans did indeed often make themselves ridiculous by becoming furious when Africans failed to understand their excruciatingly incomprehensible orders. Again and again we heard the story of the memsahib reduced to screaming by her servant's failure to act on her utterance, "Nakwenda", that she thought meant "Go now" but in fact meant "I am going". A variant of this story had the woman, half-educated in Swahili, saying with great emphasis "Mimi nakwenda" ("I, I am going").

As Mboya well knew, Africans found all this greatly amusing. They also had other emotions anxious to spring up fully armed from the rich soil of real or imagined personal and racial slights. The official said that he had himself been present, not long before, at the back of a crowd of several thousand Africans whom Mboya was addressing in Swahili. Having worked the crowd up into a considerable excitement, Mboya had then dramatically asked any African present who had ever been insulted by a European to raise his hand. Every African in the crowd had shot his hand up. Was I to believe the official? The moderate, reserved Mboya I had called on had certainly seemed capable of much more than he was allowing to show that morning. When I heard that other African politicians in Kenya mistrusted not only his Western style but his aura of concealed ambition, I knew something of what they meant.

In later years we saw more of Tom Mboya. Once, as we shall see in the last chapter, I invited him to lecture at the college, and he came. The three East African governments did their best to stop him, then argued that if he were to be allowed to lecture, against their wishes, we should restrict him to trade unionism and not permit him to wander into "politics". That trade unionism, despite its being so new there, was an unavoidable part of East African politics seemed to escape them. Mboya came and talked about what he knew, in English. As I had learnt to expect, he could not have been more diplomatic in public about general politics. Another time, when he was in Kampala on trade union business, he came to tea with us in our garden. He was affable, urbane. We talked about anything and everything that could not be considered politically serious. That evening a colleague told me that he had watched a well-dressed African hiding in some bushes just beyond the hedge near which we were sitting with Mboya. We wondered if, as our informant assumed, this was a clumsy attempt at police surveillance, with the observer observed. Equally, the man might have been some other sort of spy, or even a shy friend of Mboya's waiting for him to finish his tea. In any case, we hoped the man had found our anodyne conversation to his liking.

The last time we saw Mboya was suitably ambiguous. A mutual acquaintance brought us word that Mboya was in Kampala on business, would be in a certain night club late that evening, and would like to see us again if we could meet him there. We were quite ignorant of Kampala's night clubs and somewhat mystified, but we drove down to the address in the hot night. Outside the club it was very dark and stank of urine. In we went to find dim lights, sleazy tables, and a large tank of tropical fish. Mboya was with an apparently merry party of Africans, men and women, in a corner. One, with a gesture typical of women in Buganda when they are embarrassed, was hiding her face behind her fingers. Mboya shook his head very slightly when he saw us and gave us the faintest of smiles, which we interpreted as, "Can't afford to be seen sitting with Europeans".

Later he came over, glad to see us but had to explain, he said, that he could not spend time with us; he had his own party to look after. He excused himself specifically from asking my wife to dance. So acutely uneasy was he under the politeness that we assumed he must be afraid of the consequences of being photographed dancing with a European woman. But what might those consequences have been? Purely political? Was there a simpler explanation? Had he in fact invited us to meet him there? We stayed only a short time. He waved goodbye as we left.

On that first visit to Kenya, from Nairobi I went up into Kikuyu country, towards Mount Kenya, to call on the District Officers and raise with them some of our students' problems. Everywhere the pressure of population was evident. It was easy to understand that the men of this energetic, intelligent, disputatious tribe had gone out and made themselves indispensable at the lower levels of numerous organisations in Kenya, for example on the railway and in the post office. By the time we left East Africa, the Mau-Mau troubles largely over, I had seen on all sides in Kikuyuland evidences of thriving agriculture and small service businesses, of capitalism under creation, in fact.

On that first occasion, however, it was women's position that struck me most forcibly. As elsewhere in East Africa, the long-established practice of polygamy was of central importance to the Kikuyu economy. A man dispersed his wives about his scattered land holdings and made each responsible for cultivating her territory. While he was away doing a job in Nairobi, say, or otherwise occupied, the women continued their traditional task of raising the children and farming. That they were actively engaged in heavy work was immediately evident from the great number of them to be seen carrying amazingly large loads, often of firewood, by means of a leather band over the forehead, the load resting on the back. Bundles often dwarfed their bearers, for Kikuyu women resembled neither the tall and elegant Nubians nor the shorter and substantial Baganda. Generally they were short, sturdy and lean, their figures the result of and adapted to hard labour. As they trudged along the roads in their leather aprons they leaned far forward with their burdens. In the evening the whole countryside was suffused and scented with woodsmoke from their cooking fires.

A couple of years later I asked a Kikuyu student at Makerere, who had mentioned that he was looking forward to getting married soon, if he had ever considered marrying a girl from another tribe. He answered at once that he would find that impossible: such a girl would not smell right. I thought I knew a little of what he meant as I remembered the woodsmoke of my first visit to his homeland but for him there must have been a more complex recollection.

On later visits to Kenya I was shown the newly-constructed, enclosed villages (some called them concentration camps) built by the Government. Certain Kikuyu communities were required to move into them. The stated purpose was to protect villagers from Mau-Mau pressures and vengeance, for most Mau-Mau murders were of Africans. An unstated purpose, of course, was to restrict movement of any who might be committed to the rebellion already. Long rows of symmetrically arranged, round aluminium huts stretched out on cleared land inside the high, barbed-wire fences. The Kikuyu unfortunates forced to live in them found these huts impossibly hot during the day. Their own traditional houses had been far better adapted to the climate. A further, very serious difficulty, I was told, was that a man was expected to live with all his wives and children in the one hut. This affront to Kikuyu morality was great, the domestic strains all too imaginable.

Another policy, described to me with great enthusiasm by the District Commissioner, that affected the traditional polygamous arrangements was the scheme to consolidate Kikuyu land holdings. Instead of a man's owning a parcel here, another some way off, and a third near neither, a local committee enabled him voluntarily to exchange some of his land for someone else's, with the aim of leaving everyone with more or less the same total amount and quality of land as before, but consolidated. The purpose of this immensely complicated operation, undertaken with enthusiasm, patience, and the best of intentions by District teams, was to make it easier for Kikuyu landholders to introduce small-scale mechanisation, for example cultivators, and generally to farm more efficiently. The Commissioner, obviously a thorough and fair-minded man, proudly showed me his impressively complex maps of landholdings before and after. By the time we left East Africa there was already evidence of the scheme's beneficial economic effects. Possibly polygamous tact also somehow prevailed.

A man who owned no land at all, because there was no longer enough in the Kikuyu reserves to go round, could normally not afford even one wife. This was the desperate condition of far too many Kikuyu. They might work as casual labourers for other Kikuyu or a few might find jobs elsewhere. Most would drift in and out of Nairobi's dangerous slums, sleeping where they could and picking up whatever scraps of a living came to hand. Such men and their discontent made fertile ground for Mau-Mau. Correspondingly, women without husbands, consequently with no land to cultivate and subsist upon, found a livelihood of sorts most easily in prostitution. The majority of Kikuyu passionately supported a single, comprehensive solution for this bundle of problems: open up to Kikuyu cultivation lands hitherto reserved by law for settlers, land that in certain cases was not in agriculturally productive use. On the other hand, some Kikuyu and all government officers realised that traditional practices that had led to over-cultivation and over-grazing in the Kikuyu reserves had already caused serious erosion. More land, even if accepted as part of a beneficial policy, would not of itself cure bad African farming. On the contrary, it might delay reform of stubbornly maintained but now outmoded traditional practice. The essential was to raise Africans' standard of living above its age-old, precarious balance between subsistence and hunger. Whatever changes were made would have to be long-term and should produce lasting results. Knowledge, political patience, time, racial goodwill on all sides, these were what were most needed: none was adequately available to the colony's Government, which now found itself, confusingly, sometimes hampered, sometimes helped by its District Commissioners' necessary freedom of action as they faced the great variety of regional and tribal differences, and the requirement of working with and through local chiefs, a long-standing British policy.

It was during a later visit, to Tanganyika, at the time of a meeting there of the three East African Governors, that I met Evelyn Baring, then Governor and Commander-in-Chief of Kenya. Makerere had been having problems with the East African Governments, and vice versa. Baring wanted to talk about them. We sat privately in an inner garden courtyard at Government House, Dar-es-Salaam. I had been keen to meet him because of stories that were circulating about his calm resistance to the more extreme demands of some settlers. They were urging him to take violent punitive action against the Kikuyu as a whole in reprisal for Mau-Mau murders of Europeans. I must have asked him about these stories, for one such, illustrating his refusal to be panicked into over-reaction, he told me that day himself.

One morning a crowd of angry Europeans had arrived without warning at Government House in Nairobi and demanded to see him. He had sent down word that he would be delighted to receive them, but in an hour: meanwhile he wished to finish the passage of Virgil that he had begun reading just before they were announced. If they found that unfortunately they could not wait, perhaps they would make an appointment for another day. His appearance as we sat in the garden was as austerely composed and patrician as his style.

My inner sceptic was urging me to note also that what he had told me was theatrical, as though even he had been infected with a refined version of the Kenya swagger that early settlers had affected. Yet he could not have been more sympathetic to African education or more perceptive in judging my character. With mild but gratified surprise he said at one point, "I see. All you wish to do is work for African education."

This was an accurate comment but it also revealed that other people in government believed and feared, mistakenly, that Makerere's role was revolutionary in some more directly political sense. He offered helpful, not hostile, advice, promised to intercede on our behalf with the other Governors and to instruct his own officers to co-operate with us. Both of these he did. Yet in later difficulties between the college and the three Governments he allowed his advisers and, we suspected, the Governor of Tanganyika, to persuade him again into former suspicions. When Bernard de Bunsen then went to Nairobi for a discussion with him he insisted on talking of anything but the issues, evaded Bernard's persistent efforts to get him to deal with them, and succeeded in creating only frustration where some plain speaking would probably have been helpful. Such prevarication seemed to show that Baring was ashamed of his ungenerous lapse. Or was he simply tired out after so many strains of office? By nature a victim of his own imagination and fears? Whatever the truth, he was also a gallant man. In 1959, at the end of his governorship, while he was relaxing on the beach for a few days near Mombasa before sailing for England, an Asian girl got into difficulties in the rough surf. No longer young and in poor health, Baring plunged in and saved her. A most appropriate but theatrical political finale, you suggest? Possibly, but even so that would hardly diminish its gallantry.

Kilimanjaro and Dar

Tanganyika's huge expanse, a fraction less than that of the states of Texas and Colorado together and more than half the total land area of East Africa, remained for me much less familiar than Kenya became. Yet every visit to Nairobi, at 5,500 feet, offered the tantalising possibility of seeing distant, snow-capped Kilimanjaro, at over 19,000 feet, across the vast intervening plain. Appropriately, then, when I was able to make a journey into Tanganyika, after I had made my calls in Dar-es-Salaam I went out to the great mountain: by air to Moshi, then by car up into the cool of its shady, densely populated and heavily cultivated lower slopes. There I learned from enthusiastic District Officers about the economy, particularly the coffee, introduced in the twenties and by the fifties a cash crop abundantly grown on the middle slopes. I stayed at the hotel that formed part of the new, modern headquarters of the Kilimanjaro Native Co-operative Union, a highly successful, prosperous organisation for coffee growing and marketing run entirely by Africans save for its first secretary, A.L. Bennett. When I called on him he explained that he had now retired into the position of Economic Adviser to the KNCU. In fact, his involvement in schemes for the future was far wider than that title suggested. He gladly showed me, for example, detailed correspondence on his plan for a theatre-cum-cinema to seat 890. A history of the Chagga people (the tribe that lived on Kilimanjaro, having withdrawn there, probably, to escape from the Masai) was another of his projects. For this he was actively building up the KNCU library (I received a list of references for Makerere). When I said – and I meant it – what a wonderful impression all the KNCU achievements made, he was delighted. Not only for that reason, I am sure, he welcomed the idea of stationing a Makerere tutor at Moshi.

He took me down to the Chagga Council Buildings and introduced me to Thomas Marealle, one of the two "Mangi Mkuus" or Paramount Chiefs, an ebullient, energetic man, very much a politician. Marealle too wanted to see a Makerere tutor on Kilimanjaro and even offered money to go towards an appointment. We must have got on well, for he had me driven in the Mangi Mkuu's official car to my next meeting and that afternoon took me himself to a wedding celebration. Two Eurafricans were getting married: I was "in" because I knew a relation of one of them. There I met various chiefs, European officials, missionaries, all very cheerful, and Andrea Shangarai, Manager of the KNCU, introduced to me by the Mangi Mkuu with, "His part in the KNCU success has been to tell Mr Bennett what to do!"

That this chief's paramountcy could extend into personal concerns and possibly not always as genially was suggested when an intelligent and educated Chagga woman, one of the few working at something other than farming, complained to me that she had failed to get the scholarship to the UK that she had had reasonable hopes of "because I was not on good terms with the Mangi Mkuu". She warned that if women were to wish to attend local Makerere classes, and she thought they would want to, their husbands would have to be convinced first to allow them; also that there was much drunkenness among the Chagga, which did not diminish with education. Any Makerere tutor would have to be most persuasive, for the Chagga would find their beer parties too easy an alternative. Kilimanjaro was beginning to sound like Britain or Germany.

I found some corroboration of this when I went up the mountain to meet the seventy-six-year-old Bishop Byrne at the Roman Catholic Kilema Mission. A lively, good-humoured, impressively simple and kindly man, he had me meet the priests of the mission and the St James' Seminary (including an African priest recently returned from Rome where he had been studying philosophy for some years) and stay to tea with them all. It was a tragedy, said the old Bishop, that we had passed on to Africans what he called the cheaper, more sordid and materialistic aspects of our civilisation. Consequently, if we wished to improve the African peoples we must first change ourselves. I heard very much the same later from the intensely serious and much younger Rev. D.C. Flatt, Executive Secretary of the Lutheran Mission. Both he and Bishop Byrne looked to Makerere for help in their struggle against "materialism". My ascetic side sympathetically believed it understood what they were saying. I liked it no more than they when unimaginative Europeans, thinking only of their own comfort, treated Africans without consideration and set them a bad example. When transported to East Africa's harsh sunshine, drunkenness, gluttony and the swarm of other deadlies lost whatever false glamour they might have had in Europe. "Boy", when hurled about with venom ranging from contempt to hatred, struck into Africans' flesh like their pre-colonial enemies' poisoned spear-tips. Even when it was used merely condescendingly Africans detested the term. Distinct from all that, my sybaritic other sought an ally in St. Augustine and rapidly made mental lists of what not to ban under such a treacherous catch-all as "materialism".

Between these two selves, reason wondered inwardly how feasible it was to chop off bits of a society and pass on only those. When cultures met and intertwined was it not, rather, more like a marriage: complex, chancy, resistant to formulae, and unavoidably facing for better and for worse as equally possible outcomes? In any case, it seemed odd to want Africans to be a sort of perfection because we could not achieve that impossible aim in ourselves. Equally strange, if one could move "above" material things, to hope to be able to guide Africans away from adopting our own culture's disastrously fertile faults of entertaining unreasonable hopes and following utopian promises. The Grail of an uncorrupted and incorruptibly noble savagery obviously dies hard. Whether Makerere could ever have measured up to such austere but confused mission standards on Kilimanjaro was not put to the test in the fifties. What with the Governor's opposition, as we shall see, and the shortage of money for even primary education (which the local District Commissioner understandably said must come first) it was not until the sixties that, as Bernard de Bunsen wrote to tell me, these early efforts to get started bore any fruit.

All the Chagga people were in the KNCU, from the two Paramount Chiefs down through the subordinate chiefs and headmen (the Mangis) to the lowliest members of the tribe. Each family grew coffee and sent it to the co-operative. This unity of the tribe behind the KNCU no doubt contributed greatly to its success, but there were other favourable factors. I heard the Chagga sometimes criticised for being too parochial, too rustic and self-satisfied. In fact, it seemed to me, they had good reason to prefer their life on Kilimanjaro to the dubious advantages of towns. Clearly they were not inclined to turn their backs on a good business deal when they saw one. Nor did they wish to abandon their effective agricultural practices or forget that they had already worked them out for themselves before Europeans arrived. Nineteenth-century explorers had found the Chagga enjoying the benefits of their own irrigation system, one that made the best of and protected their well-watered slopes. At that date they already practised mixed farming, including the sensible (but in traditional East Africa most unusual) precaution of keeping their cattle in stalls instead of letting them trample about and cause erosion. In the 1950s they were growing maize on the lower slopes, coffee on the higher (not, of course, up in the belt of dense forest or on the high moors beyond), and fruit and vegetables around their houses. As a result they looked, and were, a well-fed people, with money to buy plenty of meat from their own Chagga butchers. As elsewhere, women did most of the cultivation.

At first I had found the African staff at the KNCU hotel distant, not quite arrogant but certainly rather haughtily disinclined to say more than they had to to yet another visitor, one more tourist, as they thought. When I brought former Makerere students in to lunch or dinner, however, and produced greetings from Chagga students still at Makerere, disenchantment changed to a warm cheerfulness. Relatives of some of the students came in for a chat. By the end of my few days' stay I was prepared to vouch for Chagga friendliness and to be perhaps unduly sceptical about official warnings of a Chagga tendency to political subversion. As though to reward my optimistic mood, early on my last morning there, as I stood on my balcony, the clouds that had remained thick since I arrived parted for a few minutes and revealed the glacier-covered, flattened dome of Kibo, the summit of Kilimanjaro, just long enough for me to take my tourist's snap.

How exceptional in Tanganyika was the privilege of Kilimanjaro's well-watered, fertile lands I had already discovered when I arrived at Dar-es-Salaam, the seat of the Government of Tanganyika. Its harbour some thought beautiful, but to me it looked flattened, subdued, resigned, as though bored with the relentless heat. What I learned from the Agricultural and Development staff in Dar was more interesting, although sobering. Enormous areas of the country suffered from over-whelming disadvantages of one sort or another. Here (a hand would wave over apparently all the map) the various sorts of tsetse fly were in command, carriers of diseases fatal to man, horses or cattle. These persistent insects, aided by auxiliaries such as horse flies, had gained mastery over two-thirds of the country as the nineteenth century German colonisation campaigns against African resistance reduced the population. There and there (further generous indications of great spaces), even if tsetse fly could be eradicated by prohibitively expensive bush clearance that could in any case prove only temporary, the soil was infertile or chemically unsuitable for agriculture or grazing. It would take unimaginable quantities of fertiliser and protean irrigation with unavailable water to get it to produce a bean or feed a beast.

Over great areas rain did fall occasionally but was unreliable: I gazed at more maps that showed the hazards of planting. In the centre and west, as though left over from that geological age when even Lake Victoria had dried up, 200,000 square and dusty miles were too arid for human habitation.

That was not all. Money alone would solve nothing when sufficient basic scientific knowledge had yet to be gained. Too little was known of the various soils and the best ways to treat them. What did seem to be clear was that Tanganyika was in its present condition because there lay behind it a geologically long period of erosion. Most of the topsoil had gone ages ago, leaving barren subsoils. Any remaining topsoil was thin and fragile. Even to say all this omitted mention of Africans' frequent unwillingness to co-operate in schemes designed to benefit them: they would rather go on in their old ways and ruin what little usable land there was. To be fair, I was told, it had to be admitted that recent rural development policies, handed down from Dar, had been applied so rigidly by enthusiastic but recently arrived and inexperienced British staff that African peasants had often had much to complain about.

British capital and organisation, then, were no guarantee of progress. At this point conversation always turned somewhat irrelevantly to the shamefully failed post-war groundnuts scheme. Great areas of uninhabited bush had been cleared, it was true, but at huge expense per acre. Bloated staffing by extravagant contractors had further pushed up overall costs. The planting and growing season, very short, needed good prior organisation: this there had not been. Local arrangements for supply of seed and tractor fuel to the outlying acres had often broken down. Vital experimental work had been begun after the fiasco instead of before. In the dry season the soil at Kongwa baked a hard red. It had gripped the plants and defeated the mechanical harvesters. Rains had proved insufficient, so that whatever nuts were gathered were found to be too small to sell. The scheme as a whole had been administered excessively far from base, which was in UK or Canada, not Dar. Planting in ridges, the African way of conserving moisture and making harvesting easier, had not been followed because it would have required new machinery. Another age-old African method had been adopted willy-nilly, however, for mechanisation had had to be largely given up in favour of hand labour. All this dismal story we had already heard from colleagues in the administration at Makerere who had worked in the failed scheme. They went about the Hill with an uneasy expression as though they could hear echoes of ribald laughter. In Tanganyika, too, I found it still the subject of much wry comment and sad, face-saving attempts at humour.

With all these harsh conditions explained, there seemed precious little space left on the map that was suitable for people. Down in the Southern Province there was some, by no means fully used although well watered, but that was a remote and primitive area. All over Tanganyika roads and railways were inadequate and in need of capital transfusions so huge, of such dubious economic promise, that neither government nor private concerns were likely to find such amounts. One thing everyone was agreed on was that if one day Makerere tutors were appointed to Tanganyika they would need Land Rovers to get about. Although the backwardness of the Southern Province, while beloved of the sort of devoted District Officer who enjoyed the primitive and lonely, was extreme even by Tanganyikan standards, elsewhere the best that could be said was that islands of modest prosperity stood out here and there from the dispiriting, empty wastes. Tanganyika's settlers, fewer and far less successful or politically prominent than those of Kenya, failed to enjoy an economic position that would have enabled them to set an example (in any case largely unwelcome) to Africans. Apart from coffee, sisal was the main export crop, heavily planted in Tanga Province. District Commissioners there even had serious doubts about that, as they saw land going to sisal that they judged should have yielded food. This was no trivial point, for less than 10 years back Tanganyika had suffered serious famines. Dr Williamson had his diamond mine at Shinyanga: other than that there was precious little mining. It provided an insignificant addition of wealth compared with the huge amounts contributed by the mining industry to other African countries.

In sum, it seemed to me a miracle that since the war so many new young government officers, inexperienced but energetic and full of goodwill, had continued to come out from Britain and throw themselves wholeheartedly into the vast amount that needed to be done. Despite greatly increased government spending there was still far too little money available, too few qualified men and women in any of the departments. In contrast to quietism in the upper ranks, among the young officers there survived a fresh will to cope and make a difference. All the same, I found myself wondering whether a continuation of German rule after 1919 would not have been better for Tanganyika than the forced and dislocating switch to the British spoils-of-war mandate. As soon as victorious in their ruthless nineteenth century campaigns, with brutalities severely condemned by home opinion, from 1907 to 1914 the Germans had set themselves with a will to developing their colony not only economically but in such vital social matters as health and education. In the Great War the African peoples there had remained on the whole loyal to the German cause.

The name of General Paul von Lettow-Vorbeck, commander of the Schutztruppe (Colonial Force) of German East Africa, was still remembered with awe in Tanganyika. For the whole of the Great War, with brilliant strategy and outstandingly determined and inventive leadership, he had preserved his little army as an effective fighting force and occupied the exasperated attention of the greatly more numerous Allied troops. Thus, as he intended, he prevented the latter from being used elsewhere. Territory he yielded whenever he had to: there was so much more of it available to him than supplies or trained men. Disasters he turned into advantages. In 1915, when British monitors sank the cruiser SMS *Königsberg* in the Rufiji delta, he salvaged all its guns for use by his army. Its stores went to swell the medical and other supplies manufactured locally with much ingenuity. This elusive master of bush warfare, winner of the Iron Cross (First Class) and the Blue Max, with his devoted small force of African askaris led by German officers and NCOs (both regulars and volunteers), outwitted a variety of Allied troops. British units failed to catch him. Raw Indian battalions broke and fled from his fire. Kenya irregulars and South Africans tried their hand. After a German raid on Kisii in Kenya, an outraged settler named Ross even cut off a goat's scrotum and sent it to the enemy commander with a warning that he would meet the same fate if he persisted. Somehow Lettow-Vorbeck managed to screw up his courage and shrug off this menacing recourse to white magic.

Again and again the Allies thought they had him encircled and demoralised but every time General Smuts pulled the noose tight he found his German Macavity not there. Rhodesians, Belgians and Nigerians all tried to finish him and did their utmost, but still to no avail. Even the King's African Rifles fared no better: although the best adapted to East Africa among the Allies, and most courageous, they too fell short of defeating the wily German force. When the great multi-national Allied army was sure it had him at long last on the ropes he astonished it, and appalled the terrified Portuguese, by invading Mozambique. There, with supplies for the taking, he could accept philosophically even the failure of a dramatic mission towards the end of 1917 to supply him from Germany by zeppelin: the great naval airship, confused by strange signals, turned back over the Sudan. By insisting throughout the War that his men serve, white and black, side by side as comrades, he left behind the encumbering baggage of racial distinction and discrimination. Solely because of his genius and leadership by example, through great privation his askaris remained loyal. Together, at the end a mere 1300 fighting men, 1600 carriers, and their wives and children, they held out until after the general armistice in 1918. No man or troop could have deserved more the rapturous welcome back in Berlin that awaited this undefeated German general and his soldiers in 1919. No visit to Tanganyika's wastes 40 years after Lettow-Vorbeck's heroic campaigns there would have been complete without remembering and saluting him, as had his former enemies after the war's end.

In 1956 Tanganyika was a country where the senior British colonial administrators had become accustomed to setting themselves limited objectives that might be achievable in what was, with a few exceptions here and there, a very hostile environment. That they were defensive, in spite of their conviction that caution was justified, probably resulted from the fact that Tanganyika was a United Nations Trust Territory, previously administered under a mandate of the old League of Nations after the outcome of the Great War had ended German rule there. Thus it was subject every three years to inspection by Visiting Missions, multinational committees of enthusiasts from the UN Trusteeship Council. This "interference", as they felt it to be, the British administration evidently found infuriatingly bigoted, gratuitously intrusive. The Visit of 1954 seemed to have given great offence to the colonial staff, not least because African nationalists had found it admirable. Several times officials hissed at me the name of an Indian Visitor said to be particularly obnoxious.

It was possibly this constant irritation of having to expect ill-informed criticism no matter what one did that made lunch with the Governor and Commander-in-Chief, Edward Twining, a very different experience from my conversations with Baring or Cohen. To have come from Makerere was to be thought to be like those sanctimonious, damned theorists from the UN with their heads in the clouds. Or it may simply have been that the three Governors had notably different personalities. No patrician patina or liberal aura adorned Twining. There he sat, short and stout, at the head of the dining table in his beautiful white German palace, Government House. Bristly, suspicious, looking ill-tempered, he glanced about aggressively rather like a rugby prop forward emerging somewhat confused from the scrum and hoping for someone to tackle. Yet from time to time he seemed uneasy, puzzled, incongruously as though out of depth at his own table. In later years it has occurred to me that perhaps he was always growly when hungry but that as soon as his belly had something to work on that day he might have liked to be appreciated by some modern Boswell and then possibly to purr a little. He did manage a kindly word or two before the end of lunch.

John Attenborough, Minister for Social Services, assured me afterwards that the Governor had been on his best behaviour. Others had warned that he normally bullied everyone. Yet surely he must have had admirable qualities too? Was he not the first British Governor of Tanganyika to have visited each of its districts? He was said, for example, to have supported strongly the able and enthusiastic Mr Bennett of the KNCU as well as, more generally, Tanganyika's exceptional development of co-operatives. Possibly senior government officers tended to move too cautiously and needed bullying? Certainly when Twining had first arrived as Governor in 1949 his enthusiasm and energy had been like welcome rain on Tanganyika's hard-baked wastes. Things had seemed to be looking up. Lady Twining had ably contributed her own talents for bringing diverse people together. Yet her husband's drive had come to concentrate paternalistically on the theme and constitutional "parities" of multi-racialism. Thus, when in 1954 the Tanganyika African National Union had been founded with Julius Nyerere as its President and with the Visiting Mission's blessing, the opposition between Tanganyikan African nationalism and Twining's multi-racialism had been brought to the forefront. Political initiative had begun to shift away from the Governor to his nemesis, Nyerere, who even went off into the international limelight to speak to the UN Trusteeship Council in 1955. He and Twining came increasingly to detest each other.

Perhaps, then, I should have smiled and taken as no more than a genial overture the Governor's ill-humoured comment at lunch that he regarded Makerere as a bad influence on its Tanganyikan students because it encouraged them to be interested in politics. He did not trust Makerere, he declared. It was a centre of black nationalism or Buganda nationalism (it was all the same to him, he said) and it affected Tanganyika's students for the worse. In direct opposition to Colonial Office policy he declared that he did not want to see Makerere extra-mural tutors in Tanganyika. The term "extra-mural" he found greatly amusing (I always thought it rather silly myself when applied to East Africa but in fact Africans enjoyed the formal sound of it). From time to time he sniggered away as he repeated it to himself, as though he were afflicted with a peculiarly obsessive sense of humour.

At least he did not whisper behind my back: all this came straight out. It seemed not to have occurred to him that bright young Africans might be interested spontaneously in politics and frequently in fact were, like university students anywhere. My comment that we might help them to know what they were talking about seemed too advanced a thought, even irrelevant, for a Governor beset by fears that at any moment something like the Mau-Mau rebellion might break out on Kilimanjaro. No doubt, too, he was tired from his endless battle against Tanganyika's unyielding conditions, as well as oppressed by the swelling movement of opinion in Britain against continuing with the paternal, long-term colonial approach that his whole career had convinced him was the only way. In spite of my impertinent theories about this fascinating Governor, I found him an enigma. Unfortunately I was never able to get close enough to Tanganyikan affairs to know him better before he moved up to the House of Lords in 1958. Makerere enjoyed an easier relationship with the Tanganyikan Government after he went.

Isle of Cloves

Across the narrow strait from Dar and a little to the north lay the hot islands of Zanzibar, an Arab state that flew the plain red flag of its head, the Sultan, but by treaty had tolerantly and possibly gratefully endured British protection since 1890. His Highness's Government was thus administered under a British official, the Resident, who reported to the Colonial Office. In spite of this benefit of imperial bureaucracy the town of Zanzibar itself was still divided into two by a stinking creek. On the open, Zanzibar Channel side stood the Stone Town, as it was called, with its beautiful courtyards and tall Arab houses washed most often white but other colours too (I particularly liked the saffron yellow ones), their doors palm-fringed, elaborately carved and brass-studded, some oiled and polished. There the Sultan's palace, a modern fantasy spotlessly white, asserted its respectability as though to deny that his forbears and their subjects had ever been slavers. Beyond the creek lay Ngambo ("on the other side"), the partly slum maze of jumbled shacks and small houses, crowded home to some 30,000 Africans. The whole city seemed to be foundering in the stifling scent from the godowns where great pyramids of cloves stood drying.

So it had been in December 1856, as Burton recorded when he landed there to prepare for his historic safari inland with Speke. I had arrived at the Zanzibar Hotel at noon and discovered that in that enervating climate all government offices closed for the day at lunchtime. So there was leisure to bring my diary up to date, then after the afternoon heat to walk about the town to sign the Sultan's and officials' visitors' books; also to observe, in November 1956, the changes that had taken place in the century since Burton had come there. Cloves, yes, but other features of Zanzibar that he had recorded so vividly were markedly absent. Above all, no corpses of discarded slaves rotted in the creek, food for dogs, no bloating cast-offs from the dhows floated from the harbour on to the beaches. Although I was urged to sleep under a net and remember to take my Paludrine, as well as to avoid walking through the town barefoot so as not to pick up jigger fleas or hookworm, there was no epidemic of smallpox, as there had been recently in Burton's day. Nor did cholera break out in 1959 and kill 20,000 as it had a century before. Gonorrhea, I learned later, was no longer as common as it had been when it had hardly counted as a disease, or syphilis as prevalent as when Burton had noticed missing noses and spreading ulcers. Elephantiasis, too, had been greatly reduced. Beaches no longer served as the stinking cess-pits that they had been when Burton cautiously picked his way along them.

The narrow streets of the old Arab town and the African quarter I found still odorous but not foul with refuse. Instead of the dying British Consul who urged the explorer not to venture into the perils of East Africa, I encountered next morning Julian Oxford, the Administrative Secretary of Zanzibar. Although only two days back from leave he responded in the most helpful fashion to my introduction from an old friend of his, Bernard de Bunsen. The Administrative Secretary and his staff were to be found in the largest building in Zanzibar, part of a ceremonial palace built by the then Sultan in 1883. Standing between the old arab fort and the current Sultan's palace, it was called the Beit el-Ajaib, or House of Wonders, no doubt because of its spaciousness, beautiful doors, and antique electric lift. Whatever the reasons, it would have been difficult to think of a more popular name for a secretariat full of civil servants.

Already earlier that morning I had presented another letter of introduction, to Sheikh Seyyid Soud el Busaid, the District Commissioner of Zanzibar town (there was another DC for rural Zanzibar and a third for Pemba Island, where most of the cloves were grown). Later I did the same to R.O. Williams, formerly Director of Agriculture and now Secretary of the Clove Growers' Association, whose wife was on the Educational Advisory Committee. Everywhere people received me with friendliness and consideration, from the most senior British officials and leading Arab and Indian politicians to education officers working in the field, officials such as the Chief of Police and the Port Control Officer, and the two former Makerere students, both Arabs.

I had been warned to expect much anti-Makerere sentiment, even from those who had been there, because of the allegedly widespread feeling in Zanzibar that the college did little for Moslems. As soon as I revealed, however, that I had come to find out whether Zanzibar would like to have a Makerere tutor stationed in the town, possibly a Moslem, that idea was received enthusiastically. Sheikh Ali Muhsin, still remembered at Makerere as a firebrand and reputed to be the most anti-Makerere of all, was in fact the most supportive, for he alone thought the Zanzibar Government could find the money somewhere. Everyone else, no matter how keen, told me of Zanzibar's static economy. Funds for a tutor would therefore have to be found by reducing other budgets (and, said the Director of Education, we haven't enough money even for all the primary teachers we need) or by increasing taxation. This the local politicians, for all their enthusiasm for education, would clearly be most reluctant to do. Thus I had to face the fact that unless we could obtain help from the Ford or Carnegie Foundations, or a development grant from the Colonial Office, my purpose was frustrated by the necessarily continued existence of the hospitals, dispensaries, schools and other services that had made all the difference since Burton's horrifying description.

I received charming apologies that the benign, elderly and widely respected Sultan, who had reigned since 1911, Seyyid Sir Khalifa bin Harub, GCMG, GBE, (Whom Allah Preserve, as was customarily and punctiliously added) could not grant me an audience. It had not occurred to me to hope for this honour because His Highness was not in residence. As though to console me there came invitations to lunch, dinner or tea from all sides. Several times I was taken to the English Club (members and their guests only; "officers of British and foreign men-of-war may become Honorary Members whilst stationed at Zanzibar. The Committee may extend the privilege to officers of other ships" but not, the implication was plain, to the likes of masters and mates of dirty little coasters, no matter what Masefield may have said.)

I felt fortunate to be greeted there, even if as only a fresh listener to long-held views and oft-told tales can be. At the Arab Club so many sheikhs came forward to be introduced that some had to remain nameless in my notes. There I met the young Arabs who led Zanzibar culturally and were setting the pace in political change, so much so that I heard everywhere the view (mistaken, as it was to turn out) that the future of Zanzibar belonged with them. The Asians, I regret to say, did not ask me to any of their exclusive and reputedly luxurious premises. Separate in their private clubs, these racial groups co-operated in other ways as social equals, however much they might differ politically or for the most part remain mutually indifferent racially. In 1951 there had been a serious riot, a most unusual thing in Zanzibar, given its easy-going, Moslem tolerance of differences in status and wealth. Young Arabs and Asians as well as Europeans had volunteered in answer to the urgent call for special constables. I learned that many Arabs, rich from clove growing, and Asians, dominant in trade, were far more affluent than any of the English. Significantly for the future, however, I met no Africans at all at this level. Nevertheless, there seemed to be no colour bar in Zanzibar. Parties were frequently multi-racial, shops open to all, and anyone could venture safely into Ngambo at night to witness the dances held there on Mohammedan festivals.

As happens when an outsider willing to listen arrives in a smallish, fairly remote society, people told me things about each other that they would have treated more circumspectly had they been talking to one of themselves. They revealed, too, more of their intimacies. The Oxfords carried kindness almost to excess when, not only back from leave no more than a few days but just having moved house, they invited me to lunch. I demurred, they insisted. So we three sat down, in their typical colonial administrator's house, in much disorder among half-emptied packing cases. It then transpired that they had had to engage new African kitchen staff as well. My host warned me not to expect too much. When I said why not simply some cheese his wife added with considerable asperity, "But Julian always insists on his entree!"

Her husband went on steadily and remotely with his lunch.

Elsewhere I listened sympathetically as various people revealed their fondest hopes. One sheikh told me of his plan to found a cultural association. Ali Muhsin, leader of the Zanzibar Nationalists, said he hoped to make his party even more multi-racial than it already was: he was campaigning vigorously for elections based on a common electoral roll.

On the way I picked up much incidental information: for example, that although Mohammedan law was accepted as fundamental in civil matters, the Moslem marriage system was mainly defunct in Zanzibar. While the average marriage age for Moslem girls on the island had risen from twelve to eighteen, divorce had become more frequent and made no provision for the wife's upkeep. Despite the austerity of the ruling family's puritanical Moslem tradition, morals were changing fast. Rich Arabs' and Moslem Asians' cars parked along the beach at night, as though in Florida or Texas, were hardly there purely for conversation.

Thus the Zanzibar Women's Association had such matters and no doubt much else to talk about when its members assembled on the first Monday of each month. The Moslems would come dressed in their all-enveloping, black "bui-bui" (the loose Moslem women's robe regarded in many Moslem countries as essential for modesty and protection) but only the Arabs would have their faces covered. Ladies of all races would meet in the Purdah Club as well. Mr Williams taught me much about the management of clove trees, but what I remember best is his comment that over the centuries the islanders had learnt to use all parts of their coconut trees for everything from copra to food, intoxicants and thatch. I also learned that before the British protectorate was established it had been the custom for rich Arabs, when building a new house, to immure some slaves alive in the foundations. This evil practice had led to many rumours of ghosts. No doubt such a tale, with many other folk memories, lay partly behind the appalling slaughter of 17,000 Arabs in the African uprising that was to take place one night in 1964, after the British had withdrawn from keeping the peace.

Of all the parts of East Africa, Zanzibar seemed then the least African and, because of its Arab culture, the most foreign. Its various peoples had that air of inherited, unaffectedly sophisticated intimacy of assumption and reference that marks any city that is not a mere upstart settlement. British expatriates included themselves in this atmosphere, for they told me again and again how special a place it was. They seemed generally to be well informed about its history and proud of the fact that it had one, no matter how sinister. Unpredictably, this feeling that Zanzibar was something more than its status as a protectorate helped me stand back from my educational proselytising and ask myself what I was doing. As though to reinforce my self-questioning, on my last morning there, after I had taken my tourist's photographs, peered into minute dukas or craftsmen's workshops and bought some locally made, clove-pattern silver coffee spoons, I chanced upon the long, silent protest march of black-robed Arabs carrying banners denouncing Britain, France and Israel for their part in the Suez crisis. My normally patriotic but undemonstrating temperament found itself in sympathy with the marchers. That was the experience that finally turned me away from going back to live from time to time in England, as we had hitherto believed we had every intention of doing. Now we moved towards selling our house in Chipping Norton. Without our realising it Africa had been weaning us from accepting as necessary the previously unquestioned. Canada's peacemaking was more to our taste; we began tentatively to look in that direction for our new home. Many years later, when we met Lester Pearson, formerly Canadian Prime Minister and critic of the Suez operation, we told him this story. Pleased, he sparkled again in his retirement as he must have in his youth. No doubt he was thinking what odd ways there were of reaching a decision to emigrate.

Jobs for Africans

My initial travels made it clear that Makerere needed an Appointments Service. My secretary and I started one in our spare time. We needed no budget and were able quickly to achieve a gratifying amount. We found that government departments all over East Africa were crying out for qualified Africans. Typically of people who are shifting from one culture into another, who are therefore without relevant family connexions or guidance on what kinds of career are open to them, Makerere undergraduates often had little idea of what they wanted to do after taking their degrees. In their ignorance of other openings many assumed that they had to become teachers whether or not they wanted to. To those in agriculture, forestry, medicine and veterinary science their subsequent path was usually clear, but general arts and science students faced many more possibilities than they were aware of. In particular they had failed to consider openings in business, and were at first disbelieving when I was able to suggest some. Eric Lucas, Professor of Education, raised with me his serious misgiving. Was I encouraging students not to become teachers? And was that not a disaster in a country so much in need of teachers at all levels? It was a dilemma to which there was no easy solution. We parted amicably but each unconvinced, he to contemplate the immense problems inseparable from his responsibility, I to justify again, to myself, my efforts to open up to a few the possibility of careers other than teaching.

Exploratory letters to large firms operating in East Africa and to government departments brought immediate and cordial replies. Yes, they would be glad to offer this or that well-paid job to suitable Makerere graduates. Could I suggest anyone? They would be glad to come and interview candidates at the college. The Shell Company, in particular H.C. Kewley, showed foresight and enthusiasm, but it was not alone. On subsequent journeys I was able to extend contacts in business and government while going about my other work. Eventually there was the great pleasure of seeing graduates obtain appointments in business; in the less well-known government departments, too, for example the Hydrological Survey Departments, unglamorous but highly important because whatever water there is in East Africa is constantly evaporating, often at an annual local rate exceeding that of rainfall: conservation and control of water flow are vital. Of the various things that I had the freedom to turn my hand to in East Africa, this rudimentary, amateurish appointments service, very personal and not at all bureau-cratic, gave me the most direct satisfaction, of collaborating with African students as they moved into what we all hoped was to be their new life.

Chapter 9   "Elephants Have Right of Way"

Kenya's Highlands and Coast

Makerere required its expatriate academic and administrative staff and their families to take three months' leave in a temperate climate every 21 months. This was generally asserted to be necessary for health, perhaps truly, but it was a reason scoffed at by Kenya settlers up in their Highlands and, more to the point, in Uganda by the White Fathers. These latter, the Roman Catholic chaplain was proud to assure us, were allowed to go on home leave at the end of ten years' service in their mission. On their return to East Africa they stayed for life. But, Protestants muttered, those White Fathers had an easy time of it: no career problems or family worries, no income or debts to increase, a relaxed pace of work. It was even rumoured that some of them, with all these sore advantages, took to drink. Such controversies dragged on: the real reasons for Makerere's rule on home leave remained. It gave good judgment at least a slight chance if everyone got right away regularly from the Hill's hothouse atmosphere, from the constant demands on the imagination of the adjustments between cultures, from the staff's obsession with East Africa's obdurate problems. Home leave was also necessary for keeping up to date in whatever one did or for making and maintaining contacts in the Houses of Parliament, with journalists, or in the Colonial Office, contacts needed to counterbalance the sometimes excessive enthusiasms of or discouragements by the East African Governments.

Possibly the strongest reason was that in a land without British seasons regular home leave created a pattern and that was how it had "always" been.

In between these home leaves everyone took a brief East African holiday from time to time. Our own practice was to set off before first light with Nyesi and the children so as to get a good part of the journey over before the main heat of the day. The night before we always made quiches to eat in the car for breakfast. What a never-failing but nonetheless vivid pleasure it was each time to be driving away from the Hill and leaving it there for a while with all its problems; to be going out into other parts of East Africa, all referred back to Makerere, naturally, but now to be seen at first hand, to be known from other viewpoints. Officials, settlers, businessmen of all races, professionals, missionaries, or African teachers, chiefs, politicians or union leaders, all were ready to give us their opinions, share their hopes and plans, complain of frustrations, try to have us carry back to Makerere their own understanding of matters close to them. How far to travel and where to stay were always questions. We knew colleagues who had ventured as far north as Ethiopia or down into the Rhodesias and then South Africa, but we had to consider the children above all. Of course, we never again went to stay at Masaka, where Charles had become so ill.

Kenya seemed a healthier choice. Some friends recommended Crampton's Inn, near Kitale, as suitable for a few days. It had a different atmosphere from Makerere's, they said. This, we soon found, was certainly true. The usual collection of bungalows with a central, low building for the dining and other public rooms, it was set in open, spacious grounds at more than 6,000 feet above sea level. Over extensive views of the valley, it looked away to where the broadly-based mass of the extinct volcano, Mount Elgon, gently sloped up to 14,000 feet under its enormous sky. Elgon, we learned, was possibly the anglicised form of the Masai name for the mountain, El Kony. Here at Crampton's the air was agreeably less oppressive than in Buganda. The soaring light, far clearer than down there among the listless banana trees, opened our mood to excesses of optimism, so much so that briefly we even imagined ourselves settling in this beautiful, invigorating country. For children to play on, in the grounds there was a trolley set on track, simple but popular; for everyone, a large swimming pool. The various sorts of people whom we met at this inn were the entertaining part of it for us, however, and the most interesting of all was the rangy proprietor,

Crampton himself, such a contrast to what we had become familiar with at Makerere. Then, too, it pricked our sympathetic curiosity that he was a lonely man, lean with anxieties, as we could see, for their repetition had worn deep furrows in his restless face.

He was not greatly concerned, he told us, about what might have been the causes of the Mau-Mau rebellion. He simply wanted to see it put down vigorously since it threatened Europeans' survival in Kenya. But no need to worry at his inn, he hastened to add: none of his staff were Kikuyu. We had noticed nevertheless that the staff looked not at all cheerful as they went about their work. The colony's Government in Nairobi was soft on the Kikuyu, of that Crampton was sure. Not a man given to tactful reticence, he told us candidly that he did not trust Makerere either. To educate Africans was the right thing, and he was all for it, but what were we teaching them? No point in littering the colony with unemployable BAs. Give them useful knowledge like agriculture, forestry or medicine. When we pointed out gently that some of our students were being so trained he was still not satisfied. In fact he needed to make his point in another way. What he was most uneasy about was a vaguely foreseen menace to his way of life, the coming generation of African politicians.

By the time we met him he no longer put any trust in the future. His grasp of its shape may have been unclear in its detail but his unease was specific in origin. It revolved around his powerful feelings of property. To have settled there legally and paid for his land, to have built up his business by hard work, but now... A government official, he told us, the District's Labour Officer, had written recently to say that he was coming to visit the property. So the unhappy-looking staff had complained, we thought, and it had been the Labour Officer's duty, but a thankless task, to come and speak for them. Crampton had met the man at his gate on the appointed day and frightened him off with his shotgun. With fanatical eye he told us that he would not hesitate to shoot if any Labour Officer came back. We found it not at all difficult to believe him.

Clearly, too, his feelings of property were closely connected with Europeans' continuing in Kenya. As he sat with us by the pool one afternoon, his back to the mountain, he remarked with evident pleasure that Charles already had the shape of a man. Not merely an innkeeper's flattery, this, for the sight of our sturdily active child had started in this anxious and apparently childless man, who felt himself about to be betrayed and abandoned, a momentarily happier mood, a hope that things might go on in Kenya as he had known them. For a minute or two his face smoothed over with a look of youth, or as he would be when he died.

From this frontiersman's inn we were able to make expeditions among the farms around and some way up the flanks of Mount Elgon. The small country town nearby, Kitale, proved unexpectedly fascinating because its dusty main street looked more western American than English. Among the professional men working there was a European dentist whom we were glad to visit because in Kampala it was impossible to find one who would treat Europeans for a reasonable fee. Makerere people saved up their toothaches for home leave or drove off with them to Kenya. One dentist in Kampala who would have treated us liked to drive about in one of his two Rolls Royces. It is always prudent, everyone would agree, to keep two so as to be able to lend one to visiting royalty (as he did to the Queen Mother when she came to Uganda) without putting oneself out. Richard Livingstone, who had to go to him during his stay with us, commented with Oxford-Platonic unworldliness that instead of owning such expensive motors he should have reduced his exorbitant charges.

One year we ventured as far as Mombasa, on the Kenya coast. Having driven in stages all the way there to arrive at the last by crushed coral roads lined with palms and to sleep sweating under nets at the Shanzu Beach Hotel, we found it far too hot to do much. How disappointing to discover that for a strip along the water's edge the Indian Ocean was indistinguishable in temperature from the air on the beach. It was like swimming in a hot bath. At least there was the stimulation of sharing it with poisonous man-o'-war jellyfish.

What we did enjoy was the old harbour beneath Fort Jesus, built by the Portuguese at the end of the sixteenth century. During Mohammedan festivals it still flew the Sultan of Zanzibar's unadorned red flag to show His Highness's continuing but tenuous suzerainty over a coastal strip of Kenya. Crowded with sea-going Arab dhows still using it as a half-way port on their trade-wind voyages from and back to India or Arabia, the old harbour looked much as it must have for centuries. The lateen-rigged dhows sailed down, as they had for nearly three millennia, on the north-east monsoon with cargoes of carpets, chests, dried fish and roofing tiles. When the south-west trades set in they left again, no longer slavers but full of mangrove poles and, if sailing from Zanzibar, cloves.

A very dark-skinned Arab sailor, not as villainous-looking as these crews' reputation, was offering a few characteristic baskets for sale on his deck; like obedient tourists we boarded and bought a couple.

Despite these exotica, our judgment of the coast (as a place for holidays, that is) we found to be the opposite to that of settlers from the Kenya Highlands. For them, accustomed as they were to the cool, frequently cold nights of their altitude, the coast was the unvarying steam bath where they felt they had to be for a regular spell. There, they claimed, they relaxed from the nervous effect, their degree of madness as they liked to call it, of living up in the Highlands. We, on the contrary, found sultry palms and sea level airs enervating. Except for a few inches above the water we could hardly breathe, so heavy were the heat and humidity. A trio of young European men walking in bathing trunks along the beach looked grossly overdeveloped and over-fed compared with the more modestly built but fit African fishermen. These latter we enjoyed watching as they manoeuvred through the surf in their dugout canoes with outriggers. Far out at low tide we found reef-pools but also discovered how dangerously fast the returning, rippling waters flooded in, as with Charles on my shoulders I trod what I hoped were the ridges of sand as the ocean swirled about my chest. Baking on the beach left us feeling unwell instead of refreshed. The climax of excitement was the children's sandcastle competition, especially arranged to divert fathers. Not our sort of holiday. We longed for nothing more than to be back in the Highlands and active again.

More to our taste was another country hotel in Kenya, back at a cooler and lighter elevation of nearly 8,000 feet. At Kaptagat, a convenient "half way" point between Nairobi and Kampala, Captain T.A.C. Pakenham, RN retired, a man in his fifties, and his wife Clara had made an hotel, the Kaptagat Arms, on a beautifully treed property. Since they lived there and managed it themselves it was well run without sacrificing that attractive Kenya air of makeshift about the buildings and facilities. To arrive in the early, pine-scented, already voluptuously chilly evening after the day's drive in the heat, after one's sweating back and neck had been tortured by the corrugations and one's hair stiffened with dust, to find a wood fire lit in one's bungalow bedroom and, in the primitive, adjoining bathroom, peat-coloured hot water that smelled of woodsmoke from the makeshift boiler outside was doubtless not the noblest form of bliss, but for an hour we all voted it superb (Charles's favourite word at the time: "superv", he pronounced, as he played in his bath). Blankets at night added to the pleasures of change, as did next day the sight of horses, which could not be kept at lower altitudes. Fair exchange, we thought, for mosquitoes, so plentiful down there but too feeble to manage the flight up.

For the innocent there was a golf course. Put aside notions of cunningly positioned hazards between closely mown greens, O pampered, effete legions of civilised, conspicuously-consuming golfers. Think instead of Scottish moorlands where the game began, where rough meant nothing less than rough. Then continue to stretch your imagination in that direction until you reach what you shudderingly recognise as an appalling, nightmare picture of unbelievably rough. You may now have a pale idea of the Kaptagat golf course. "Golf carts or caddies?" you idly ask as the reality stubbornly eludes you. Even the direction in which one was supposed to drive the ball was far from clear, because greens were not in sight through the exuberant growth between, and were in any case not green but brown like everything else. Captain Pakenham had smiled enigmatically and murmured something about working generally eastward. Such problems were minor, however, when compared with one in particular. For half way out we encountered an erosion gully across the course. By gully do not understand some small cleft or even a large crack in the earth's surface. Imagine a gulch a couple of hundred yards across, and with no bottom in sight. Well, not quite the Grand Canyon but a fair imitation and an admirable spot for snakes. Another odd thing, we noticed, was that nobody else was playing. Could that be because of their disinclination to meet a rhinoceros, we began to wonder. At this point we decided to make our way back. No panic, just a steady trot. Had we thought to bring a compass we should not have been late for lunch.

From the hotel we made expeditions out into the country, most memorably to stand one day, ourselves alone save for an African in a tattered overcoat, on the precipitous lip of the Rift Valley, to feel the warm, sweet-scented updraught and look down across the immense, brown floor into a distant haze. In the foreground the light was so clear that the few clouds seemed to hang up there stationary and definitive, as though they alone were truly clouds, the originals of Magritte's.

One evening we were invited to dinner by settlers in the locality and heard the latest Mau-Mau gossip. They also told us that Mrs Pakenham was well-liked because always ready to write to the Lord Chamberlain on behalf of settlers who hoped to have their daughters presented at

Court. Next day the Captain was anxious to know if they had said anything about his hotel. Could it be that settler neighbours did not always see eye to eye? In fact, he now confided to us, he and his wife were trying to sell the hotel but buyers were hard to find. He felt no more confidence in a future Kenya than Mr Crampton had had. Yet the Captain's case was different: social position and naval self-discipline constrained his expression of views as well as what he hoped to do. Not for him the outspokenness of an old settler, the unconventional Anglo-Irish trader, R. Gethin, who had come to Kenya in 1908 and was glad to leave in 1958 with the boast that he had the satisfaction of taking out and transferring to South Africa and elsewhere £38,000. No shooting at official intruders, either: instead, up anchor and slip silently away on the darkling tide. All the same, no matter how discreet the departure of such a personage, with his connexions in the peerage, it would be noticed, would cause tremors among Europeans who remained. Once seen, with his star-gazing, nautical eye and trim, grey sailor's beard, his aura of having seen active service in the Great War, then in 1939-45 of having made the Murmansk run through dreaded, icy waters, he would not be forgotten. Moreover he had been marked in a singularly public and decisive manner.

He did not much like Nairobi, he told us, but when the young Queen and the Duke of Edinburgh had come there after her accession he had decided to go down to Government House for the garden party. In the grounds the usual large circle of guests had gathered. He had taken up a position at the back, as inconspicuously as he could manage (he was perhaps a little under average height). The Duke made his rounds, spotted him at once, had him come forward to shake hands, and exclaimed, "What the hell are you doing here?"

The Captain, we then learned, had commanded a ship in which Prince Philip had served at an early stage of his naval career. The Duke's question struck us as most apt. It was precisely one, taken more generally, that we too wished to ask. There had been aristocrats before in Kenya who had run hotels, some merely to satisfy their need to be rowdy, yet this case was far from that. When at last we found the opportunity to ask the Captain he took evasive action and put out a smoke-screen of mutterings about retirement, not going to seed, either this or Holy Orders, and re-potting being good for... but we never did hear for what as he gave us his charming smile of authority and moved off to resume command of his ship-shape hotel.

With the Lepers in South-Western Uganda

For those who wanted to spend a holiday in Uganda the Ruwenzori Range in the west, along the border with the Belgian Congo, was always being recommended. So we saved up to make the journey to Fort Portal, but the night before we were to leave I hurt my back so badly that even to sit in the car was impossible. With the money, instead, we bought a small picture from a travelling French exhibition (during our six years in East Africa there was only one such and one fashion show: operas, ballets, orchestras flew over us *en route* for Salisbury and further south). Bernard de Bunsen, always the Buxton Puritan (his parents would keep a little sherry in their house for visitors, he would say), disapproved of those of us who made such purchases, said "extravagance" gave an impression of our having too much money, a sumptuary stricture from which Persian rugs seemed to be exempt.

We felt consoled for having had to miss the Ruwenzori when we heard later that these "Mountains of the Moon", with peaks well over 16,000 feet, revealed themselves in their mists only rarely. The arduous trek up beyond Fort Portal gave no guarantee of seeing them. Their exotic plants, including the famous giant groundsel and giant lobelia, required stiff climbs before they could be inspected. We decided that, after all, the Ruwenzori would not have been quite the place for young children. Not for adults either, necessarily, since a colleague who developed pneumonia while climbing had died up there. Swiss mountains might have hospitals and shelters aplenty but there was nothing tamed about the Ruwenzori.

We did, however, make the journey down into south-western Uganda, almost into Ruanda-Urundi. After we had been at Makerere for about a year a colleague decided that we had been working too hard. She obtained for us an invitation to stay for a few days as paying guests with medical missionaries, Dr Sharp and his wife, on Sharp's Island in Lake Bunyonyi, near Kabale. There they had established a hospital and colony for lepers, under the auspices of the evangelical Church Missionary Society.

Down there in the Sharps' guest house we felt and were a long way, in both distance and spirit, from that semi-Europeanised Africa of holiday hotels in Kenya. During the day the lake reached all around us in a placid, silvery hush, as though nothing could ever disturb it under its shelter of clouds. At night the silent cold seemed to suck us down into even deeper isolation. The Sharps had been there for 30 years. They had chosen this uninhabited island and made it their home, had altered their immediate surroundings by building their bungalow and making a garden, but in doing so had inevitably been absorbed into the isolation. Apart from the nursing sister at their leper colony they were the only Europeans living there, the only ones for several miles around. They seemed to enjoy their self-sufficiency, took pride in their solitude as in an achievement. It certainly was a world apart from Makerere, where at any hour of the day or evening someone might arrive at the steps of our open house and call "Hodi!" ("Anyone at home?")

On another island, out of sight, stood their life's work, the leper colony and hospital, also built from scratch. The thought of the lepers somewhere out there, their disfigurement and sufferings unspecified but all the more strongly imagined, hung over us all the time we were there, followed us about like a remembered threat while we did our best to relax and amuse ourselves.

One mark of our remoteness was that we renewed our acquaintance, first made at Masaka, with what was called throughout East Africa "the Kenya lavatory". Dating from the long ages before sewers or septic tanks, it consisted of a large and terrifyingly deep hole in the ground with a seat across the top of it. As Dr Sharp told us, given that the hole had been dug deep enough initially, the resulting pile at the bottom decomposed so that either the hole never filled or the level rose so slowly as not to be a problem during one's lifetime. In such facilities one might find a pot of lime from which to throw down a scoopful to keep the monster below under control.

One evening, when they invited us to dinner, we listened to Dr Sharp's lamplight tales of his regular hunting safaris. He was in the habit of going off for months at a time to camp in the wilds wherever the hunt required, sometimes in Uganda but more often across the border in Ruanda or the Congo: not, then, the familiar sort of missionary. As he spoke there were mysterious hesitations as though he were recalling experiences that we should not understand or might not sympathise with. Could he possibly have been comparing himself with an earlier English hunter, Charles Stokes, a missionary turned trader, summarily executed in the Congo Free State by the Belgians in 1895, some said for aiding Arab slavers, others for illegal possession of ivory? Was it of any significance that, tentatively, to find out what we knew, he had brought

up Stokes' name at one point? Or perhaps he was considering the implications of the fact that in Tanganyika, recently, government officers
had been sent to prison for possession of ivory.

The doctor's pauses remained inscrutable but he did give us much
incidental advice, the sort that one stores away like inherited home
remedies for dealing with unlikely emergencies. For example, never
sound your car hooter at an elephant. We had not contemplated doing
anything remotely as disrespectful. An acquaintance of the doctor's,
however, had done so when impatient to pass through a herd, whereupon a huge bull, enraged, had reared up and brought down his tusks
through the roof of the car. This had no doubt surprised the driver.
Without question it had killed him. A well-deserved fate, we agreed.
After all, he had been warned, for on our journey down, as we drew
near Lake Bunyonyi we had seen a roadside notice, evidently not new:
"Elephants Have Right of Way". This sign had brought to mind the
explorer Baker's hair-raising account of being pursued in 1863 and
almost caught by a great bull elephant as he spurred his horse desperately to escape. Our sympathies were with the animals, for Baker, the
foremost big-game hunter of his day, had wounded the elephant
mercilessly and brought it at one stage to its knees. And all for sport!

In view of the slaughter for ivory to which many Europeans had
looked to supplement their incomes up to the Great War (not to
mention much later), we judged it a proper tithe of revenge that of the
10 Europeans (apart from missionaries) in Kampala in 1903, one had
been killed by an elephant. The doctor's hunting trophies seemed
more genteel than ivory for income, but they were prominently
evidence of something. He had had coffee tables made from whole
elephant ears, tapering triangles six feet long, and most uneven their
surface was, more suitable for robust beer steins than delicate coffee
cups. We dared not ask if elephants still grew tusks as well as ears.
Instead we did our best to respond to the Sharps' enquiries about
conditions "at home" but it was difficult: their remembered country
seemed different from ours. They proved less well disposed towards
African education than we had expected. In fact, their views on
Makerere were similar to what we were to hear later in Kenya from Mr
Crampton: educated Africans were a threat because they had been
taught the "wrong" things.

During the day we had for distraction the choice that our host had
matter-of-factly put before us. Since we were on such a splendid and

beautiful lake, he thought it obvious that we should want to amuse ourselves in a boat. We could either try our luck with his dug-out canoe or take a chance with his sailing boat. The latter, he told us, he had built himself with galvanised iron over a wooden frame. It had no buoyancy tanks. If we dumped, it would sink. The lake, he reassured us, was very deep. Lifejackets? He looked puzzled: no, he had none, not as far as he knew! Only soft Makerere people, afraid of drowning, could possibly need such effete supports, his back seemed to suggest.

We debated our intriguing choice. My wife reminded me that as a boy I had paddled a canoe on the children's pond in Regent's Park. This I could not truthfully deny but I did think to suggest that she might possibly recall her canoeing lessons on the river at Oxford, where St Hilda's College, clearly over-civilised by Bunyonyi standards, insisted its undergraduates try not to drown. In the end it was decided, by whom was not clear, that since I had flown aeroplanes I should be able to manage the dug-out.

The doctor called for it. An elderly African in an ancient khaki great-coat paddled it expertly to the dock. He jumped out and politely held it for me to get in. Whereupon, precariously seated, I looked along it for the first time and noticed an oddity. The canoe was considerably curved. Perhaps trees did not grow straight at Lake Bunyonyi? Dr Sharp called out that one had to find its balance. It was not that I disagreed with him. I even fervently wished to do as he said: but there was a further problem. The dug-out rolled. Not "if one did something silly" or "if one leaned over too far" but constantly, as a matter of course, simply because all logs roll. How I was to find its balance when I would be under water was not at all clear. What it needed was a pair of Mombasa outriggers. In spite of shifting about I could find no steady way to sit. In the air, it is true, I had performed slow rolls, snap rolls, loops, Immelman turns, and so on, but the relevance of flying to paddling dug-outs was now ignominiously proved to be zero. Somewhere, no doubt, the wilful creature (for clearly a tree spirit was still alive in it) had a centre of gravity, but deep down in the water it must have been, an erratic point shifting about like some unreasonable particle. Amused, the boatman helped me out and, unsung genius of balance that he was, removed our choice by paddling the unstable beast away. My advice to any person contemplating tropical adventure would be to prepare long in advance an unanswerable excuse (unexpectedly called away to a Masai lion hunt?) in case threatened with ordeal by dug-out.

Reduced to the doctor's lethal, hardly Hippocratic alternative, we sailed sedately back and forth a few times one day in a light breeze to show willing, then retired to our guest bungalow to prepare our delicious dinner. That morning we had shared with the Sharps in the expense of having a kid slaughtered. We found that it had not been divided lengthwise: our half, it turned out, was the scrawny front. With no refrigeration to deter the billions of bacteria, local wisdom decreed that the meat be eaten the same day. That evening a further revelation was vouchsafed to us. That exotic delicacy, Lake Bunyonyi kid, is renowned the world over, or certainly deserves to be, for being exquisitely tough. How, we wondered, can the wretched leopards and pythons keep going on such a diet.

The prospect of the leper island was still with us when our few days on Sharp's Island were almost over. I decided to face the dragon by asking the doctor to take me with him when he next went over to the colony. It was the Sharps who insisted I go alone with him: an unsuitable place, they said, for a small boy. My wife was not reluctant to stay behind. The doctor and I set off in a motor boat. On the way he told me diffidently of his problems in getting his hospital started, of winning Africans' confidence, of making do for years on slim grants from voluntary contributions in Britain to the CMS (supplemented, possibly, in this good cause, by another, mysteriously unmentionable source of income?) Yet he had evidently enjoyed persisting and using his ingenuity.

Then we landed. He was a changed man: it was as though he had entered his fiefdom. There was no doubt who had established the place and kept it in order. His will had prevailed and the patients were grateful to him for it. It was a relief to find that I could mingle with the afflicted without any of my anticipated horror. Dr Sharp made it easy for me by not letting me see the worst cases. Most of the people I shook hands with, those moving about as if in a village, had no overwhelming deformity, lacked no major part of themselves. One man had lost his nose. A woman's hands were badly swollen as though she were suffering severely from arthritis. As a community, however, they looked, and I believe were, by far a happier and even healthier lot than the lost souls whom I had seen a few years before when, as an elected member of the Eastbourne County Borough Council, my duties had included visits of inspection to a mental institution. Those I had found deeply distressing. At Lake Bunyonyi I felt only respect for the doctor's and sister's life-work, and above all for the patients' African stoicism in the face of all-too-common hardship or disaster: ask for little, expect less, for "Shauri ya Mungu" ("It is God's will" or "Leave it for God to worry about").

Since it was a Sunday, at the appointed hour we all walked, limped or shuffled into the church. That is, we gathered on long benches under a large roof with pillars supporting it but otherwise open to the air all round. This structure was quite undecorated: the money had gone into other things. Dr Sharp led the service. The nursing sister played the harmonium. It was a suitably simple occasion and all the more moving for that. Only the hymn-singing brought it home that this was no ordinary village. Plaintive, mournful, its tones, whatever the words, told of families left behind, of a sinister disease. Long-winded at the best of times, the Bantu language now seemed particularly in its element. In prose or conversation the difficulty of saying anything succinctly in Luganda or a similar Bantu language seemed not to matter much as long as time was not pressing, but here, with the hymns, it gave rise to bizarre musical effects. "O God our help in ages past" went the familiar first line of the melody, played slowly, to which the organist added po-o-om, po-o-o-om on the humming harmonium to allow time for the African translation to catch up. "Our hope for years to come," tiddly pom-pom she went on, deliberately. So it continued, every line. No bracing, optimistic, muscular Christianity possible here with dirgeful hymn singing like that: rather, "From the tombs a doleful sound". Think of a melancholy, slow "All things bright and beautiful" p-o-o-m, p-o-o-om, and you may begin to imagine yourself looking out over serene, silvery Lake Bunyonyi from your idyllic place of confinement, the leper island.

"Out" and "Home"

In the fifties, travel by air to and from East Africa was changing fast. We were just too late to enjoy what all who had experienced it described as the ideal way to "come out" or "go home". This was by flying boat, in leisurely stages arranged according to the aircraft's range and the stretches of water suitable for take-off or landing. It worked out that one flew only by day. At night passengers slept comfortably in hotels *en route*, relieved not to have the roar of propeller engines battering their heads. Among those who had travelled on these great aircraft, nostalgia

obliterated the memory of noise and left mythic tales for the bemuse-
ment of latecomers. The cabins of these flying boats grew in the telling
until, with their upper and lower decks, we imagined ourselves wan-
dering about them at will as though in the Verandah Café and Palm
Court of the *Titanic*. The bar, so we heard, was the scene of day-long
conviviality. If these stories were even half-true those must indeed have
been three-day-tipsy journeys. We had just missed, we were assured, the
perfect compromise between the rapidity of air travel and the amenities
of civilised conditions. In more prosaic 1953 we had to endure a journey
that, by flying day and night with stops only for refuelling, dragged us
by propellers from London to Entebbe in 24 hours. During our six years
in East Africa we saw the introduction of propjets, faster and less noisy
than the earlier engines but still not quiet. The revolutionary jet, the
Comet, raised hopes with its brilliant passage then dashed them with
its tragic disintegration.

The alternative to air travel, to make the journey by sea, was still
open to us in the fifties. We used it twice: in December 1954 on the
British India Steam Navigation Company's SS *Kenya*, making its established run from South Africa to London via Mombasa, and in the summer of 1959 on the Lloyd-Triestino line from Mombasa to Trieste. One
needed time to do this: the journey to London took three weeks. Up the
east coast of Africa past Somaliland, a stop at Aden, through the Suez
Canal, stops at Port Said, Malta, Marseilles and Gibraltar, then the Bay
of Biscay run home, it was still in the last few years of Empire a wonderfully evocative way to go. Somerset Maugham, Conrad and
Masefield jostled their words and images through one's senses as one
sized up fellow passengers and was judged and placed socially oneself
in the ineradicable English fashion. In first class we dressed for dinner,
naturally, but not first night at sea – trunks not unpacked, you see – and
not on Sundays – it's only supper, don't you know; the formulae, well
rubbed, repeated generations of talk.

There was the traditional quota of eccentrics and bores. Menus still
Edwardian offered long sequences of courses and generous choices
within each. Even so, one young bachelor whom we found at our table
astonished us by making it a declared point of principle, repeated at
every meal as though a ritual incantation, to eat as many choices as
he wished within each course. He must be satiated soon, we said, or
perhaps he will explode; after all, even the Romans could not have
kept up that sort of exhibition without a vomitorium. Yet keep it up,

rotundly, he did. He had no conversation, literally no time for it. His manner of eating was singular: self-confidently furtive, self-righteously dedicated, and fast. Eat up, eat up, he would urge us. Since it is true that one way to a man's heart is through his stomach, we confidently but erroneously expected a burial at sea. Only once did he fail to live up to his principles. It was when he and I were among the half dozen passengers at dinner at the height of a severe Levantine storm. Prudently he confined himself to a meal that could have lasted most people a week.

Then there were bores to avoid, particularly one ravaged-looking physician who could be seen confiding to anyone who would listen his certainty that our consumption of sugar was the root cause of Britain's decline. This news he gave with a dark, mysterious look, with many preliminary hints and nods, as though his victim were forcing the truth from a reluctant witness. When he finally came to his revelation he looked hurt, betrayed, regretful, as though aware that his oratorical talents fell short of what his momentous conclusion deserved.

Deck games remained as fatuous as they had always been. Mid-morning on the British India Line, as if passengers were invalids in need of constant nourishment, Asian stewards moved among the deck chairs with cups of consomme.

We "crossed the line": the hoary ceremony in the sun had much of the feeling of a damp Guy Fawkes night when long-promised fireworks splutter disappointingly. One thing that did live up to expectations on the SS *Kenya*, however, was the ritual of the bath. Bathrooms for men were hidden in a row behind a gloomy ante-room where a sour-faced Asian bath steward presided. Women's baths were somewhere else, safely concealed from the shipboard proclivities of ogling males. After a chat, our Asian custodian turned out to be a sad, efficient and pleasant man who cleaned the bath for one before use, ran the water, and with ceremony ushered one into privacy. There a great surprise was waiting. The bath water was from the sea. Soap would not lather in the salt. One came out feeling stickier than when one went in.

A day out of Mombasa, Charles went down with measles. We expected it. The evening before we were to leave Kampala he had felt unwell. Our physician thought it was going to be measles and said he had better give him an injection to delay the illness long enough to get us to Mombasa and safely on board. He administered whatever it was, Charles slept most of the way in the train, and we boarded. Next day we were not surprised when he was banished into quarantine in the sick bay at the stern. There, fussed over by the ship's British nurse and kindly Goan stewards, he spoke English to the nurse but the Goans he puzzled greatly by insisting on addressing them in Luganda, in which by this time he could manage within his needs. "What language is this?" one of them asked.

Most of our time we spent with Charles. Although the reason was unwelcome, while not particularly distressing for him, it proved the unanswerable excuse for not joining in this or that version of mutual torture indulged in by our fellow passengers. Far from bored in what was in practice our private sick bay suite, for Charles was the only patient, we were happy to have the time to enjoy his company and, when we steamed through the eroded Greek islands, to try to remember for him some of the traditional tales from ancient days when those scorched, bare hills were well-wooded.

The Lloyd-Triestino journey was different in several ways. The crew and ship were Italian, the ship itself newer and brilliantly white, the cabins and public rooms more elegant. Bathrooms in the cabins obviated the need for the British India ritual of the bath. On the way up the east coast of Africa we dropped anchor off Mogadishu, the capital of the Italian Trust Territory, Somalia. Goods and baggage for shore had to be lowered into small boats that had come out into deep water to meet us. A gay, hit or miss air prevailed as the apparently feckless local boatmen, Arabs probably, with a vigorous sea running, soared and plunged like shrieking sea-birds. In fact their skill was so assured, their cries all part of their expert performance, that they managed the trans-shipment without loss. Then came the disembarking passengers' turn. The game was to lower them one by one in a sickeningly swaying basket to be grabbed by a sailor below, his hand now within grasp, now vertiginously beyond reach or hope. As they stood by the rail awaiting their turn in the stiff breeze, these disembarking wretches had the desperate expression of candidates for the guillotine who see their fate ahead of them. Yet all was safely accomplished, to general cheers.

Charles, now almost eight, and I left the ship at Port Suez to travel overland to Cairo and the pyramids while my wife stayed with the infant Julia. We were to meet again at Port Said. In the desert between Port Suez and Cairo it was 120 degrees Fahrenheit. Over the city as we approached in the evening hung a huge pall of hot fog. Next day we were tourists, and in the evening were supposed to rejoin the ship. In fact, between our leaving Port Suez and arriving at Port Said, dramatic events had occurred on board. Of these we knew nothing. What we could see for ourselves was that the ship was not at the dock. Without explanation we were taken in a launch, now in the dark, to the outer harbour. There was our elegant liner. But it was steaming along and not slowing! With much shouting the launch drew alongside at a point where a platform had been let down from the ship's side. In the opening and on the platform a score of the crew stood crowded together, arguing and pushing. The men in the launch made their craft fast to the platform, whereupon one of the liner's crew drew a knife and proceeded to cut the rope. Others struggled to restrain him. I wondered what we could possibly have done to deserve such an operatic welcome back. For lack of an answer I moved Charles quickly up into the bow, managed to hand him to an enormous sailor who leaned out to help, then jumped for the unstable platform myself. Only when we were all four reunited did we learn that while in the Canal the Lloyd-Triestino crew had voted to go on strike. The captain had then refused to dock, reasoning that a strike at sea would amount to mutiny, a far more serious matter that the crew dared not risk, while on a docked ship it would be merely a strike.

So we resumed what was to be a gloomy voyage. As one would expect from Italians, the stewards remained courteous even though underneath they were smouldering. One told us what the crew's wages were. It seemed to us a disgraceful pittance, and our sympathies were with them. Our tickets were to have taken us only as far as Venice; given the captain's decision to dock only if unavoidably, he steamed straight for home port, Trieste. We mere passengers were left to wonder if we should be allowed to disembark. We watched Customs officers being kept off while an argument raged on board. Some crew members stood by at the hoses ready to repel boarders, the decks already wet where they had tried out their armament. Eventually a peace of sorts must have been agreed; we were graciously permitted to carry off our own luggage. What good fortune that all our packing cases and removal trunks were on another ship. Our last sight of the crew was of further violent discussion, but whether it was proof of discord or harmony we could not tell as we set off for the train back to Venice.

Chapter 10 Time to leave

It was early in 1959 that the Chief Secretary of Uganda, the senior minister under the Governor, came to dinner at Makerere, on high table in Northcote Hall's great dining hall. A huge man of quick rages, Charles Hartwell had a large head, red face and a long, bulbous nose that threatened to grow altogether out of hand. He sniffed, as was his habit, shudderingly. His ugly, kindly, honest face emitted a voice normally loud but that on occasion could roar. When he wanted to see his assistant in the secretariat at Entebbe he was said never to use telephone or buzzer but simply to yell, as though for a minion, at a volume that could be heard all over the building. Aptly, he was nicknamed Kali Charlie, "kali" in Swahili meaning angry or fierce. In fact, as I got to know him I found him quite human. My secretary, Neta Jones, a mature judge of character and well placed in Kampala expatriate society to obtain information, told me that the talk had him far more capable than the Governor. As a senior member of Hartwell's staff in Kenya had said of him to me before he was promoted to be Chief Secretary of Uganda, "Nobody could be more fair-minded than Hartwell".

So I found him. Under his noise there lurked an active, well-intentioned administrator: intelligent, reasonable, not at all petty or pompous, and in his own way good-humoured. After one of his rages he had discovered his secretary in tears, whereupon, appalled, he had dropped state business to rush out and buy her a large box of chocolates: banal, Hollywoodish, but definitely endearing. Americans, I noticed, were terrified, and disapproved of him.

Hugh Dinwiddy, the warden, tinkled his little, ornate brass bell with claws around the clapper. All remained standing for the brief, creedless grace with which dinner began daily, a formula that I had carefully negotiated in 1953 with Catholics, Protestants and Moslems: nobody seemed to care about the closet animists. Guest night had brought out 30 or so members of high table, sweating in black gowns, their guests in dark suits, Paul Foster the only exception in his severely white Dominican habit, the keen, inquisitorial glance setting an edge on his smile. The 200 or more students had dressed equally formally: each wore his red gown. They looked up at high table on its low dais at one end of the hall, most with respectful amusement, a few with a youthful hostility far more complex, less tolerant, but all with the curiosity appropriate to the inspection of a familiar but separate caste. The long, polished mvule table that they saw, reaching the width of the hall, could not have been more solid, or the matching chairs, red leather-seated and -backed, heavier to move.

A large, silver rose bowl, presented by the Secretary of State for the Colonies, decorated the centre of the table. In the body of the hall waiters in white kanzus rushed barefoot in and out. They brought food in large aluminium sufurias, battered cooking pots with lids that rested insecurely rather then fitted. The same, but containing different food, were delivered sedately to high table by its own waiters, distinguished by green kanzus with red cummerbunds and fezzes and by walking solemnly, as they had been taught by the domestic bursar. The juxta-position of dented aluminium and silver rose bowl was much deplored by a faction among high table members which had been urging that only silver appointments could be appropriate. Others of us enjoyed the incongruity. We all looked apprehensively at the sufurias, given our distinguished chief guest, for mistakes could occur.

The last time Andrew Cohen had dined in that hall, in 1957, at the end of his governorship, a chocolate sauce had turned out to be brown gravy, cold and thick, when poured on Lady Cohen's steamed pudding. This evening, however, there were neither mistakes, as yet, nor visible cockroaches. We settled down in relief to an agreeable occasion. The hall was rapidly becoming even hotter and cheerfully noisy. A ground-nut soup had just been served. One of the lecturers could be seen fur-tively cleaning his spoon with his gown. I was sitting opposite Hartwell, who was on the warden's right. The talk was relaxed and lively. In good humour, the Chief Secretary smiled and bantered. Then my neighbour,

Dr Allbrook, perhaps tactlessly asked me how long I thought it would be before Uganda became independent. Hartwell heard the question and was alert. Others nearby paused to listen. Possibly even more tactlessly but in the open spirit of the conversation so far, I replied at once: "Three years," I said.

It was to prove an accurate prediction, but to judge by colleagues' faces it seemed then an outrageously short estimate to those who heard it. Its effect on Hartwell was Wagnerian. He flushed and frowned, looked angry and frustrated, raised his enormous fist and crashed it down on the table. Plates bounced and rattled all along. "If it weren't for people like you encouraging Africans," he roared to high table at large, "we'd be here another 25 years!"

He was not alone in the general tendency of his opinion. A mere five years before, with Tanganyika's independence then in fact only seven years off, the UN Visiting Mission to Tanganyika had thought 20 to 25 years would be a reasonable target for the trust territory's independence, an estimate that Julius Nyerere had accepted at the time. More recently still, in January 1959, the Secretary of State and the East African Governors, conferring at Chequers, had proposed even at that late hour to contain African nationalism for another 10 years. Cushioned sedately in their chauffeured Daimlers, they had failed to hear the speedy future revving up to overtake them with news of their imminent capitulation.

The hall was hushed at Hartwell's outburst, but when I smiled at him after a tactful pause he resumed his earlier self, his quick storm spent, and Hugh Dinwiddy was able to restore urbanity. The students took up their talk again even more excitedly. I had given my prognosis purely clinically, so to speak. That British rule, in Uganda but also in East Africa generally, would be coming to an end so soon I did not now regard with enthusiasm. It seemed more cowardly than responsible to hand over the lives and welfare of our African friends to no matter which thugs and incompetents might collar power behind a deceptive smoke-screen of "democracy". Such fears of submerging a grasp of local conditions under some political slogan of a general transfer of power I had already expressed in a letter to *The Times* back in 1954. Rather, traditional British empiricism, I had argued, "should guide us... to an appraisal of each separate colonial situation". In some cases, I had suggested, a timetable for the transfer of power might make sense: in others it could lead only to disaster. The argument, by 1959 commonly heard among East African intellectuals of all races, that self-government would redeem its probable mistakes, that it was better for an African to be treated no matter how badly by "elected" fellow-Africans than to be governed by a colonial power, no matter how well, seemed to me likely to be severely tested by the probable enormity of those "mistakes". For given human depravity as a constant, self-government in abstract could surely not be an aim of any value. Yet as Kali Charlie's outburst showed, it was the movement of opinion and slackening of will in Britain that had left the East African colonial Governments far behind and unfairly presented as mired in a shameful past. When Richard Livingstone, born in 1880, had come out to stay, he had commented to us, regretfully but accurately, that a career in the Colonial Service used to be regarded in Britain as a noble calling but now was looked down upon as indefinably base. Hartwell had probably felt himself under pressure to hasten his government's departure, but a man of his experience and honesty must have had a clear idea of the costs to the African peoples of so doing. Two crises in the relationship between Makerere and the East African Governments had already underlined some of the tensions in this tragic situation. They had brought out painfully the three-way differences in outlook between government, university, and opinion in Britain, not to mention the gulf of endless prejudice between each of them and that great illusion, the fabrication called world opinion.

The Extra-Mural Department at Makerere was set up in the fifties, at the Colonial Office's request but with the college's warm support, with the same broad intentions as had guided the creation of similar agencies in Britain during the latter half of the nineteenth century and since. That is, of extending in various ways the university college's influence and activities out to such members of the general population as cared to benefit and could do so. Annual summer schools had long been an accepted feature of extra-mural programmes in Britain. Oxford had held its first, one of the earliest, in 1888. They brought into the universities for a week or so people of all sorts of occupations, most of whom had been studying throughout the winter in classes in their towns and villages. Makerere's small new department, funded by the three East African Governments and supported by substantial grants from the Carnegie and Ford Foundations, decided in 1957 to try some-thing along these lines.

In lands without clear seasons it could not call its venture a summer school. Instead, it hit upon "Annual Study Vacation", which inevitably became "the ASV". From the start it was to be open to applicants of all races from all over East Africa. In the absence of any other suitable *lingua franca*, proficiency in English was the passport. Extra-mural classes at that time were still few in this enormous and predominantly harsh region, with its 18 million people and three-score main tribes. Huge areas, including the whole of Tanganyika, had none. Yet the ASV seemed a good opportunity to bring in African teachers and others of some education, whose intellectual isolation out at their posts could hardly be exaggerated, and give them a chance to learn a little realism about their countries' problems and prospects. This policy, it seemed to me, was right, for how otherwise could anyone even begin to break through the multiple defences of provincial ignorance and prejudice in time to be of use before "democracy" descended? How else to ensure that even elementary knowledge of the condition and needs of East Africa, as distinct from current political slogans such as "Freedom!", might be spread about instead of staying confined in official heads and files? Thus there would be seminars led by Makerere faculty as well as lectures for all by ministers and senior officials of the three East African Governments. Agricultural, health and economic experts from the Colonial Service would also teach. Invitations to attend the ASV went out to numerous organisations of all kinds, and for each race, to be passed on to their members. Advertisements appeared in the East African newspapers and on the wireless.

To say that this scheme worried some officials in each territory would be like saying that monarchs in Europe at the end of the eighteenth century were mildly disturbed by the French Revolution. Files grew fat as official letters rapidly became acrimonious. Secretaries and typewriters overheated. Governments tried to dictate what could and could not be done: pleading academic freedom and responsibility, together with its mandate from the Colonial Office, Makerere resisted. Correspondence style at that time required letters to be long-winded, seemingly with an eye to some celestial recorder who would one day pronounce a judgment called history. Many and protracted were the meetings. People stopped among the peaceful greenery of the Hill to exchange "the latest". The three Governors met in special conference at Entebbe to discuss the situation. Each was perturbed (it was revealed to us later that Uganda was undergoing a "security drive", whatever that might have meant) but Twining in particular huff-huffed furiously at what he saw as politicisation of his supposedly apolitical Africans.

Bernard de Bunsen, summoned into the Governors' presence, found himself threatened with an accusation of having acted in bad faith: he had asked me to accompany him, and I saw him for the only time looking drawn and distressed. Twining insisted that he would be sending an official observer to the ASV. On the Hill people muttered "spy", a term not altogether fanciful since we had direct evidence of Special Branch reports on Makerere classes held off the Hill. The college replied that of course anyone might apply, save that all places were already filled. This created an apparent impasse that further diplomatic effort finally resolved. Even after the ASV had taken place reverberations continued to shudder through many sheets of correspondence. The event itself, as the college confidently intended, proved to be gentle, good-humoured, serious-minded, innocent, with every place taken. Africans, with a few Asians and Europeans, came from all over East Africa. The college showed its own flag by giving a garden party in their honour, which the Governor of Uganda, Frederick Crawford, graciously attended. An embarrassed, pleasant European official introduced himself to me as "the spy from Tanganyika". By entering into the spirit of the occasion he seemed genuinely to enjoy himself. We invited him to tea in our garden where any residue of misplaced suspicion could be eased away. Later he wrote generously to say that he thought the college had done the right thing. Perhaps he reported the same to his superiors.

Since the Governments continued to rumble menacingly, however, as the time came for us to go on leave, Bernard de Bunsen gave me the job of quietly lining up support at home. He suggested I start with Godfrey Elton, originally a National Labour peer but by the fifties an Independent in politics. When I sent him papers to read he invited me for a chat, remembered that Lucretius has a celebrated line about the pleasures of looking on at other peoples' troubles from a distance, but did offer to "utter something" in the Lords should the need arise. I gave lectures at three universities. A group of MPs ensured that Hansard recorded supportive comments. John Grigg, at that date still Lord Altrincham, who had heard of our difficulties from his brother, wrote to request an article for his *National and English Review* and invited us to dinner to press his interest. I had to decline his offer and explain that Bernard thought a public row at that stage would do more harm than good. I briefed other journalists and asked them too not to publish: they did not. Opinion at the Colonial Office and the Inter-University Council, and in senior academic circles, that is, among the members of the Atheneum, was discreetly but actively sympathetic. All that anxiety, argument, heat and posturing over a "summer school" in countries soon to be independent! Such was the common attitude among those sophisticated experts in survival.

Christopher Cox, Educational Adviser at the Colonial Office, was particularly acute in grasping the essentials of both Makerere's and the Governments' problems. In spite of his frenetic timetable and apparently hopelessly chaotic desk (at which he dashed off barely legible longhand letters to all those "far-flung" outposts), not to mention that his clothes seemed to have been made for someone else and pulled on in desperation while his razor was scraping some areas of grey stubble on his cheek but missing others, he managed to fit in two long, private discussions with me and remained a penetratingly sympathetic correspondent. By tradition, he emphasised, colonial Governors enjoyed considerable independence from London.

After probing carefully to be sure that Makerere was not about to land him in embarrassments similar to those created for him in West Africa by Thomas Hodgkin and his left-wing Oxford associates, he assured me of his support. Cox still talked of "the Cause", that is of education and liberal policies generally for the colonies, but by now he spoke the word with a lift of irony, a hint of wry self-reproach.

The memory that remained alive for us after the dust had settled was above all what we and Lalage Bown had seen at Kampala railway station at 7.00am on the day most of those coming to the ASV by rail from Kenya and Tanganyika were to arrive. As the train pulled slowly in, Africans were leaning far out of the windows: some were right outside the carriages, hanging on. When the train stopped a great crowd surged off, tired and grubby, carrying cardboard suitcases or bundles, but excited, cheerful, looking about as at a fresh day in a new world. We welcomed this one or that; anything more was at that point impossible. The most moving thing of all was when one African teacher from a remote part of Tanganyika told us he had been travelling for three weeks. Makerere students confirmed later that this must have been true, so delayed were the connexions that he would have had to make.

Not long after we returned from leave the college received a request from the US State Department, forwarded by the Colonial Office, with its support, through the secretariat at Entebbe, for a private course to be held during the long vacation, 1958. Its purpose was to familiarise a group of 20 or so United States diplomats with East Africa. They would come to the Hill for three weeks and learn whatever the college judged they should be taught, in whatever way it thought best, as long as there was an appropriately wide representation of political and other views. After leaving us they were to suffer the same sort of thing in Southern Africa, then in French and Belgian areas. These were to be not diplomatic cadets but officers already in Africa or about to be posted there. Their *chef de mission* would be Fred Hadsel, but the most senior in the group would be W.H. Taft III, an officer with the status of ambassador. No costs were to fall on the college. Thus, innocently enough, were sown the seeds of the second crisis.

This official request, impeccably presented, was received on the Hill as an enlightened gesture by the State Department and not less by the Colonial Office. It was turned over to the Extra-Mural Department for action. Among the East African Governments, however, strong feelings were expressed that here was an example of Americans thrusting themselves forward before the Empire was dead, let alone the corpse cold. Why, it was asked with pompous pauses into dictating machines as the typewriters started to fill the files again with carbon copies, should Makerere take it upon itself and put itself out to help them at all? Messengers sped to and fro between the Hill and Entebbe. My wife, carrying a missive from Bernard de Bunsen to the Governor of Uganda, to be delivered to him personally at Government House, found herself courteously invited, in the absence of Lady Crawford, to pour tea for him. There she found to her surprise that what the Governor really wanted to hear about that afternoon was not arrangements for the Americans but a conference of the International Students' Union soon to be held at Makerere, organised entirely by the students. She told him plainly what a low opinion we had of some of the foreign delegations expected, particularly the Algerians, because they had been disturbing our Makerere students with their violent letters. When this group of histrionic student politicians arrived on the Hill a few days later one of the Algerians, a very "mature student", told her that he had been surprised at how frightened the Makerere group were to receive his heart-warming advice on "how to get rid of their colonial masters: use piano wire to garrotte them!" Evidently he despised such unpromising candidates for revolution. Through all this brouhaha the Extra-Mural Department went ahead and drew up the sort of programme that the State Department had requested. Distinguished speakers were to lecture on a broad range of East African subjects, the history, economy, peoples, politics and social problems of all four territories. Various ministers and senior government scientists gladly accepted invitations to speak. That Kenya's politics were to be covered not only by members of the Government but also by settler politicians (Michael Blundell and Humphrey Slade) and, gasps from some, Tom Mboya, by now a member of the Legislative Assembly, certainly gave rise to adverse comment in recesses of the Kenya Government.

This second "crisis" was nevertheless mainly a Tanganyikan concoction. The draft programme suggested government speakers on Tanganyikan politics but also, to put another side (that there could be no other side seemed to be the Twining doctrine) the most prominent African politician in the Territory, Julius Nyerere. He would not be allowed to leave Tanganyika, came the irate cable in code; he had been banned from making public speeches. But he had been provisionally invited to this occasion – this private occasion – and had accepted, was Makerere's response. Was Tanganyika, a United Nations trust territory, prepared to tell the Americans that they must not listen to a leading African who had already addressed the Trusteeship Council in New York? Further questions implied: was it proposing to go on accepting money for adult education from American foundations without giving back this small help to American diplomats trying to inform themselves about East Africa? At an opportune moment the State Department applied discreet pressure. In the end the Tanganyika Government gave in. Grudgingly, Nyerere was to be allowed to attend and speak, but a minister of the Tanganyika Government was to be present when he did so.

The Americans arrived, all white as it turned out. From the start they could not have been more tactful or less troublesome. Some were immensely tall and presumably found the students' beds in the hall of residence excruciatingly short, yet requests for changes were muted as though it were an offence against diplomatic propriety, if not indecent, to be so much taller than Africans. Early on one of them brought me after breakfast a small envelope. In discreet silence he opened it and held it up for me to see inside. There I observed an unfamiliar little insect about which I expressed polite interest to this, as I supposed, amateur entomologist. "A bed-bug," he whispered.

The food, too, they manfully tolerated. Through lectures on more about East Africa than they probably wanted to know they sat in the heat with admirable fortitude. With every appearance of content they suffered through the garden party that the college gave for them. Yes, Buganda was hot, they allowed politely, but Washington in summer was intolerably humid: they should receive a tropical allowance when they had to work there.

It was not until the speakers on Kenyan politics arrived that the Americans showed by their excitement where their main interest lay. They followed the Kenya lectures breathlessly, absorbed in the various and on many matters opposing points of view of Africans, missionaries, government, and the divided settlers. When, at the end of those days, faced with the task of summing up, I compared the situation in Kenya, that we had just seen so vividly displayed, with the inevitability of a Greek tragedy, the tension of satisfaction was extreme. That part of the course, at least, they might remember. Before that, in the Tanganyika section, Nyerere had spoken, but disappointingly dully and emptily for a man reputed to be charismatic. Perhaps he had found the minister's required presence intimidating? After all, when the minister arrived, stout, late and flustered, he had discovered Nyerere already taking afternoon tea in the common room with other lecturers and the Americans. In loud irritation and with a very hostile stare at Nyerere, he had asked, "What's he doing here?" Then he had added, by no means *sotto voce*, that Nyerere had been indicted on charges of criminal libel.

Whatever the truth of that, the impression Nyerere had left behind was of a charming man who unfortunately had thought little about anything other than the most rudimentary political machinery. While able to state impressively that the future Tanganyika would be a home to citizens of various races who would however vote on a common roll, he had had nothing specific to say on the enormously difficult questions of economic and social policy. About the implications of African nationalism as opposed to tribal or regional interests he had remained equally vague. The contrast between the competence, freedom, range and spirit of the political speakers from Kenya and the constraint and immaturity of those from Tanganyika had been striking.

My wife and I gladly entertained the Americans at a sundowner that went happily save for an unfortunate moment. We had invited various people, among them a recently qualified Muganda lawyer, to meet the Americans. Standing with his drink in a circle of them, this young man said, "Take any chimp, give him a fridge and a radio, put him behind the wheel of a Cadillac, and you've got an American!"

Appalled silence. After a diplomatic pause, Fred Hadsel said quietly to his colleagues nearest him, "Maybe we should reconsider some of those grants we're giving."

As for ourselves, we found the Americans refreshing. In spite of their obsession with Foreign Service hierarchy and concentration on their prospects, and although they seemed not widely curious, not free spirits most of them, to us nevertheless they were new and delightful. What their course had done for us, however, was to emphasise again the fissures between the Colonial Office and the East African Governments, and between the latter and Makerere, which itself oscillated uneasily somewhere half-way between British intellectual majority opinion and East African realities. Above all, it had reinforced our conviction that British power in East Africa would now be hurrying off more hastily than had the Roman legions from Britannia. With it would go the opportunities to give the help that we had come to offer. As it had turned out, we were simply among the latecomers of Empire. The long-term assumptions upon which such an idea of helping had been based had themselves crumbled. No longer did it seem admirable, for example, that some post-war experiments begun at the agricultural research station at Serere had been planned to last a century (Serere, north-east of Kampala, beyond Lake Kyoga, was where Makerere agriculture students went for practical research experience, and objected to having to dig a little, "women's work"). More important still, a moral tradition that had come down to us from John Stuart Mill was about to expire in what we foresaw as Empire's imminent and chaotic aftermath. Into this historic rift the future for East Africa that we had at first so naively looked forward to had disappeared. Although by the end of 1958 relations between the college and the Governments had improved greatly, our new, sober assessment served to reinforce our family policy. Sadly, it was time to roll up our bundle of residual uncertainties and leave.

When it got about in 1959 that we were going to a post in Canada, Mr Kisosonkole called on us. "Please don't leave," he urged, "it's people like you that we need."

Deterioration in the political atmosphere already showed as a restless discontent. He had no better idea than we how people like us, soon to become foreigners in Uganda, could go on helping in what lay ahead. As my wife said to him, "You can't tell a rioting crowd not to throw bricks at us".

That same week, after dropping Charles off at the European primary school and with Julia aged two beside her in the front, she had driven the car down the usual street to be confronted by just such a riotous crowd kept back by African police holding up circular shields in front of themselves. She had reversed away and taken another road. A few days earlier she had experienced an ambiguous incident. An African in Protectorate Police uniform had stopped her at the base of Makerere Hill as she was driving home. "Where are you going?" After her outraged answer he said, "You are free to go now".

Gratuitously officious, merely? Orders misunderstood? Or the first stirrings of police lawlessness? At the same time disturbing rumours circulated even more wildly than usual: for example that African orderlies at Mulago Hospital had begun extorting charges for the use of bed-pans. What we did know for certain was that an Asian clerk at the post office in Kampala had demanded 7 shillings from my wife for a routine form; his Asian superior had embarrassedly countermanded this illegality when she protested. Nor could it have improved the morale of upper-class Baganda that the Kabaka's father-in-law was told by the Governor, who was sleekly looking the part at our Makerere garden party for the Americans, that he hoped there would be "no trouble" during the remainder of his term of office. For, the Governor had added, "I have boys at home at boarding school".

My wife and I were standing with them. We were embarrassed, surprised, appalled that Crawford should reveal and spread his nervousness and poor morale in this way. Given that there was soon to be, we were sure, a transfer of power, let it at least be orderly and confident, as Africans in fact wanted. A jumpy occupant of Government House, remote from everyday dealings with Africans, could only make our job at Makerere harder, and all the more difficult for others out in the field. That there were already worries enough was made even clearer when another prominent Muganda, a rich coffee grower clinging desperately to the past, invited us to tea. In his well-appointed house, over his elegant tea cups, he urgently impressed upon us that we should tell the Protectorate Government people and the Colonial Office at home what uneducated rabble-rousers were leading the independence movement. Its principal figure of the day he scorned as a "one coat man".

On the Hill tempers grew shorter as clouds of anxiety, their outlines all the more menacing for being imprecise, rolled in over the future.

171

Leave, then, we believed we had to, although others, a few, would judge later that they could hang on, at least for a little while. So we began to decide on the things we wanted to take, the rest to be sold. Since there were no companies to pack our crates, boxes and trunks, we did that ourselves. How to get a Regency buffet table into a crate not made for it? My wife packed rugs tightly all around it and between the legs. Thanks to her skill it went off to the ship with the rest and came through undamaged, as did the china that she packed, the heavy, mvule chief's stool from Kisii, some delicate Regency chairs, our finely made Kigezi baskets, our pictures. The only casualties were some of the books, which still carry scars from my too-vigorous efforts to nail down lids of tea-chests securely.

It was a sadly happy time. Friends drifted by gloomily for a drink, to see how we were getting on and help manoeuvre large objects into small crates. Alisi and Nyesi were far from their usual cheerful selves: Alisi said things would be "very bad" when the British pulled out. Yet on the Hill in general the Europeans seemed encouraged that we had "managed to get away", as they put it. Colleagues who would normally have been content with "Good morning" now stopped for a chat. How, exactly, they wanted to know, had we pulled it off? Told, they would nod, satisfied. Nobody asked what our salary would be in Canada because everyone already knew. The offer had been made by telegram and that had had to be received by the Bursar's office. It sounded an enormous sum to all of us unworldly children of sterling. One naive friend told us that he had been working out from Whitaker's which exalted British officials we should equate with! Even government people congratulated us warmly: glad to see us leave? One pleasantly sardonic official in the secretariat encouraged us greatly by adding that he had once been in St John's, Newfoundland, where we were going, and remembered that the pavements were made from beaten down cinders. Another, a stranger to us, whom we had to go and see in Kampala before departure, dealt quickly and impersonally with our business, then relaxed, called for coffee, and expanded with sympathy into what we were about to do. He too, he said, had faced a similar decision a year before. His job in finance gave him too little to do. The secretariat had ignored his recommendations for improvements in efficiency. So he had decided to leave, but at his convenience, not the Government's. For the meantime, with official work that took him only an hour or two each day, he was speculating in gold on his own behalf.

How did he manage, I asked (in those days before computer links), so far from the main financial centres and sources of up-to-date information? No problem, he replied: his department had regular access to all the data he needed. Had he done well? Very, and as soon as he had made enough he would resign. Differently, a passing Member of Parliament, unconcerned with our plans for our life, vigorously expressed his disapproval of our departure, made me feel something between a traitor and a deserter, then caught his plane back to London. Bernard de Bunsen, on the other hand, said he was glad we were going to Canada because it was so much more established and developed than other parts of the old Commonwealth.

One of our sadnesses was to be leaving Bernard. As Principal, he had been such a wise, courageous and generous support through so many difficulties. Others, too, had been wonderfully supportive but he particularly and perceptively so. His steadiness and sense of humour had made him always a welcome companion and friend. He had, even more important, a sense of honour and a realistic grasp of principle that he was prepared to use his wide range of social contacts to support. Others saw him differently. Some fire-eating, "no-nonsense" types judged him harshly as too indecisive and idealistic an administrator, and, as a late and untimely heir to liberal colonial policies, effetely pro-student. Many regretted what they saw as his inadequate involvement in purely academic matters: not at all like his predecessor, the philosopher Professor Lamont, they said, who had been *primus inter pares* academically and whose office lights one could see burning far into the night as one looked up respectfully at the Administration Building. Yet what could one expect, they would continue: Bernard was a good enough fellow but not a distinguished scholar himself, a less than brilliant degree at Balliol, then his first job teaching in a primary school – would you believe it – and to have come to Makerere straight from being Director of Education in Palestine, a worthy post but hardly of academic distinction. Of course, he had had a bad start, Quakerish, sent as a boy to Leighton Park school. On this view, it was as though Bernard were a relic from the pre-war Makerere, from the now-surpassed normal school. Cutting across other judgments was the one (mistaken, as I believe) that saw him as regrettably deeply in the sectarians' pocket.

A few enviously hoped to depose and succeed him. One pair in particular, puffed with purpose, stalked about the Hill conspiratorially, now brazenly, now looking shamefaced. One even made the grave mistake when on leave of taking his ambition to the Colonial Office. By this miscalculation of Bernard's social position (as his friend the former Canadian Senator, Eugene Forsey, says in his autobiography, to criticise anyone in public life when they were at Balliol together was to run the serious risk that Bernard would say "Oh yes, he's my uncle") he succeeded merely in revealing himself as an intriguer covetous of power in transparently hopeless and fantastic ways. Others saw Bernard, with his distinctively Prussian head, only as a member of too elevated and pacifist a stratum of English society to be trusted. Was not his local bank balance a steady £9,000? Had he not gone to Berlin with a Buxton uncle just before the war in the inane hope of talking Hitler into peaceful ways? Then there was the fact of his many German relations: as rumour had it, he was still in touch with them. One man summed up his own unease, his feeling that relationships with Bernard were socially ambiguous, by always referring to his smile as "shark-like". Above all this, Bernard continued serenely.

Most agreed, whether for or against him, that he was a character. Stories gathered around him. One day he asked me how he might control his stomach's inclination to sag and spread. I lent him a book of exercises, F.A. Hornibrook's *The Culture of the Abdomen*, which first frightened readers by detailing the appalling inner consequences of living the abandoned life, then required them, a fitness fad of the time, to sway and gyrate abdominally as though warming up for Egyptian dancing. He did try a few of these exercises in the privacy of his bedroom, he told me, but had to give them up because, as he said apologetically, he felt it was indecent to move his torso about in such a fashion. We all admired his finesse in evading the snares laid out for him by various ladies on the Hill, who thought such an eligible bachelor should marry, that he needed above all the matchmaking help that only they could provide. Some men clearly thought of him as old-maidish rather than eligible. Bernard knew this, encouraged it, and enjoyed asking the mock-naive question. On one occasion he delighted in seizing the opportunity to tell a story that turned this spinsterish reputation to advantage. It was at a relaxed weekend luncheon party. In the way of meandering conversations, some of the men, talking of this and that, found themselves discussing a colleague who had had, as the phrase used to go, much success with women. "I don't know how such fellows do it," cried a reluctant and envious bachelor.

Bernard saw his chance. At once he interjected, "Oh, I know how it's done".

Some comments manage to be heard through no matter how many veils of other chat. He had now a hushed audience. "I arrived at the Norfolk Hotel in Nairobi. There was some confusion about which room I was to have but after a bit they sorted it out and gave me 26. As I was dressing a note appeared under the door. It read 'Would the lady in Room 26 care to have a drink before dinner with the gentleman in Room 14?' So I wrote on the bottom 'Delighted to – Bernard de Bunsen,' and pushed it under his door as I went down. He introduced himself later and apologised. Apparently the lady had left the hotel unexpectedly. Rather disappointing for him, but he took it well."

Bernard's freedom from pomposity and pretension was well illustrated by his dislike of, and lack of ease in, formal ceremonies. At Makerere's first degree-giving, in December 1953, he sat unhappily up on the platform, glad at the great day for the students, of course, but uncomfortable at having had to dress up in academic costume and play a part. At the end he rose a little too early, patently eagerly. Tall, short-sighted and stooped, he looked about, myopically uncertain, as though puzzled by something he had forgotten. Indeed, there was something, his mortarboard. He had taken it off at an appropriate point in the ceremony and, presumably hot, had neglected to put it on again. As the procession moved out through the hall he remembered just in time, grabbed the hat from the floor beside his chair and put it on. Normally his walk was tentative, hesitantly full of stops and starts as he talked, but now he moved triumphantly, almost jauntily, in step with the encouraging music. Unfortunately he had his mortar board back to front and paraded smiling out of the hall with the lower point of the hat down on his nose between his lenses. Stuffier onlookers tut-tutted, but most of us were delighted to see him, in such typical form, offering so spontaneous a parody of academic processions, which are a folly at the best of times.

Not long before we left, an occasion arose that yielded Bernard's most memorable comment. On the Hill at that time there lived an exceptionally lovely young African woman, one of the students. What was remarkable was that she was thought beautiful by both Europeans and Africans. Tallish, elegant, well proportioned, not thin but far from the substantial build then still generally appreciated in women by African men, this goddess walked about the Hill seemingly unaware of her distinction. She was from a feudal kingdom distant from Buganda. A couple of weeks before the end of term a message came for her that she was needed urgently at home to take part in celebrations of her king's long rule. It transpired that her role was to be conspicuous and specific. As the most desirable subject imaginable she had been selected, since this was a special occasion, to be the monarch's concubine for a week. Some said her lord wanted to offer her to another Uganda monarch, one of his guests, but the truth of this matter of the etiquette of hospitality was never made clear.

Dutifully and with undisturbed composure the student applied to be allowed to leave early for the vacation to prepare herself for whichever great honour was to be hers. If she was silently praying for help to Saint Barbara, protectress of beautiful women, she gave no outward sign. Alice Burnet, the warden of the Women's Hall, whose responsibility it was to grant or withhold permission to leave early, considered her request with intense concentration. Was this honour consistent with the morality that Makerere hoped to instil into its women? Could it be called an appropriate use of leave? If granted, would such a leave be compassionate? Did it sit well with the position in African society of women with a University of London education?

Yet if permission were refused, what repercussions? Makerere, of all places, could be called anti-African! Europeans might enviously think her king no better than an ageing lecher but in gaining this most coveted prize he would merely be confirming what his people took kingship to be largely and properly about. Did they not accept that their monarch owned all the women in his kingdom? He had only to make his choices known, to drop a necklace over this bowed, submissive head or that. In an agony over this most taxing of decisions, the warden went to the Principal for guidance. Some might have thought that an unworldly bachelor, looked at one way or another, was hardly the person to advise a spinster on such a question. Not for nothing, however, had one of his grandmothers been lady-in-waiting to Queen Victoria, or an earlier ancestor (von instead of de) Prussian ambassador to the Court of St James. After due consideration, with exquisite judgement of diplomatic compromise balanced with propriety, he gravely pronounced, "It's all right, I suppose – as long as it doesn't happen in term time". This we had delightedly from the warden herself.

The sale proceeded of things we were not taking with us. Our loud-speaker cabinet, made of mvule in the college workshops to our own design, went to an enthusiast who also bought our heavy, bronze turntable and the Leak amplifier, with its beautifully glowing valves, that worked so well despite my having had to assemble it. We decided to keep many of our gritty records since these by now provided our definitive performances. The wilder jazz we presented to the junior common room in Northcote Hall, and heard later that it was not at all to the students' taste. An Asian family snapped up Julia's pram. In the end all had been sold or sent to the auctioneer, where Ray Beachey offered to keep an eye on it for us: all except the bearskin, that is. It lay fiercely alone with its blocked head, glass eyes and mounted teeth. The evening before we were to catch the train we decided simply to leave it in the house. None of our staff wanted it. Then an African whom we did not know came out to see us from Kampala. He had heard of the bear and offered to buy it: the lion, as he too called it. We quickly completed the sale for a shilling and had the unique pleasure of watching him set off down the hill, past the anthills and through their acrid scent, with the bearskin on his back, its head over his head. Goodness knows how many Africans he frightened in the brief dusk as he walked away beneath the gleaming, golden-yellow blossoms of the cassia avenue.

So we shut the windows on our garden house and locked ourselves out, leaving its hospitable rooms forlornly to contemplate empty Morris armchairs or silently to reproach us with mattresses lying stripped and awry on the mahogany bedsteads. Next day, having spent the night with friends, we boarded the train for Mombasa, Charles and Julia solemn, Alisi, Nyesi and Abunwazi in tears as friends and colleagues waved. As for ourselves, we two were saying goodbye to more things than we could have numbered. Fresh woods and pastures new are all very well, but they do involve irreplaceable losses. Even lifelong regret can never give a full account of itself.

Index